On Writers & Writing

By Helen Sheehy and Leslie Stainton

Published by Tide-mark Press Ltd.

 New Moon   First Quarter  Full Moon   Last Quarter

Design and Typography by Corry Kaeser Cote

The Written Word

The anonymous 12th-century copyist in the Castilian monastery of Silos understood the hardship of his trade. "If you do not know what writing is, you may think it is not especially difficult," he revealed on the colophon of a manuscript. "Let me tell you that it is an arduous task: it destroys your eyesight, bends your spine ... and makes your whole body ache ...

Excerpt from the Book of the Dead

Like the sailor arriving at the port, so the writer rejoices on arriving at the last line."

The copyist's writing materials were simple: a two-sided pivoting desk, a set of goose quill pens, ink, a leaf of parchment. With these few instruments he created civilization.

It is by mastering the art of writing, Jean-Paul Sartre argued, that we achieve "the means to conquer the world."

The first "words" were pictograms. Etched onto clay tablets with a stylus, or rendered in brush and ink on a primitive form of paper, these early written communications gave way, in the Western world, to abstract symbols and eventually to letters, and in China to a complex system of characters that is still in use today.

Of the roughly 3,000 languages currently in existence, only 100 or so are written down. One in two adults cannot read. Charlemagne was illiterate; he signed royal decrees with a cross.

Writing has always been a sacred act. In ancient Mesopotamia, scribes were a distinguished caste — more powerful, at times, than the sovereign. Scenes from the Egyptian Book of the Dead, written in the 13th century B.C.E., show dead persons surrounded by passages of text whose presence is meant to ensure the resurrection of the deceased.

With the invention of moveable type in 14th-century China, and Johann Gutenberg's subsequent development of the printing press, writing reached the masses. Craftsmen like Aldus Manutius and Claude Garamond labored to create beautiful fonts using metal letters. Manutius drew inspiration for his Aldine font from Petrarch's writing.

By the mid-18th century metal pens had replaced quills. (In 1806 William Wordsworth wrote "the longest letter" of his life using one of the new, steel-nibbed pens.) Fountain and ballpoint pens followed. Then came the typewriter and word processor.

The instruments vary, but the art and the act of writing retain their magic. "I can remember things only if I have a pencil and I can write with it and I can play with it," said Rebecca West. "I think your hand concentrates for you. I don't know why it should be so."

Sunday
28

 Monday
29

Tuesday
30

Wednesday
31

Ramadan begins
Thursday
1

Catherine Drinker Bowen, b. 1897
New Year's Day

Friday
2

Saturday
3

| December 1997 | | | | | | |
S	M	T	W	T	F	S
	1	2	3	4	5	6
7	8	9	10	11	12	13
14	15	16	17	18	19	20
21	22	23	24	25	26	27
28	29	30	31			

| January | | | | | | |
S	M	T	W	T	F	S
				1	2	3
4	5	6	7	8	9	10
11	12	13	14	15	16	17
18	19	20	21	22	23	24
25	26	27	28	29	30	31

Sunday
4 *auditions / "Fantastics"*

Monday
5 ☾

CH (SAC mtg)

Tuesday
6

Carl Sandburg, b. 1878   *Dr. Vito 5pm*

Wednesday
7

Zora Neale Hurston, b. 1891   *students return*

Thursday
8

Wilkie Collins, b. 1824   *portfolio night / Jim Dayle arrives*

Friday
9

Simone de Beauvoir, b. 1908

Saturday
10

<table>
<tr><th colspan="7">January</th></tr>
<tr><th>S</th><th>M</th><th>T</th><th>W</th><th>T</th><th>F</th><th>S</th></tr>
<tr><td></td><td></td><td></td><td></td><td>1</td><td>2</td><td>3</td></tr>
<tr><td>4</td><td>5</td><td>6</td><td>7</td><td>8</td><td>9</td><td>10</td></tr>
<tr><td>11</td><td>12</td><td>13</td><td>14</td><td>15</td><td>16</td><td>17</td></tr>
<tr><td>18</td><td>19</td><td>20</td><td>21</td><td>22</td><td>23</td><td>24</td></tr>
<tr><td>25</td><td>26</td><td>27</td><td>28</td><td>29</td><td>30</td><td>31</td></tr>
</table>

January
1998

<table>
<tr><th colspan="7">February</th></tr>
<tr><th>S</th><th>M</th><th>T</th><th>W</th><th>T</th><th>F</th><th>S</th></tr>
<tr><td>1</td><td>2</td><td>3</td><td>4</td><td>5</td><td>6</td><td>7</td></tr>
<tr><td>8</td><td>9</td><td>10</td><td>11</td><td>12</td><td>13</td><td>14</td></tr>
<tr><td>15</td><td>16</td><td>17</td><td>18</td><td>19</td><td>20</td><td>21</td></tr>
<tr><td>22</td><td>23</td><td>24</td><td>25</td><td>26</td><td>27</td><td>28</td></tr>
</table>

Simone de Beauvoir
January 9, 1908 - April 14, 1986

Often, when her father had gone out to play
bridge, and her mother and sister had fallen
asleep, 15-year-old Simone de Beauvoir
would lean out the window of her father's
study in their Paris home, and peering
through his opera glasses, she would spy on
strangers. "I was—I still am—very con-
scious of the fascination of these little peep
shows," she wrote three decades later, "these
lighted rooms suspended in the night."

Beauvoir remained an acute observer of life.
Her many volumes of essays, fiction, and
memoirs offer unsparing accounts of youth,
friendship, love, death, and dying. When she
published *Adieux: A Farewell to Sartre* in
1981, the book — a record of Jean-Paul
Sartre's last months, and of his conversations with Beauvoir—shocked critics with its
blunt recital of Sartre's mental and physical decay.

To imagine Beauvoir's life without Sartre is difficult. Friends dubbed her "la grande
Sartreuse," or "Nôtre-Dame de Sartre." The two met as students in 1929. "It was the
first time in my life that I had felt intellectually inferior to anyone else," Beauvoir said
later of the encounter. Within months, Sartre suggested they sign a "two-year lease" to
signal the start of a lifelong commitment to one another. They never married. Each
maintained a separate residence. Both took lovers. Their attachment transcended the
bounds of convention.

Beauvoir shared Sartre's belief in a godless world without preordained values, a world
in which human beings are solely responsible for their actions. She vowed as a young
woman to do something useful with her life. She viewed writing as a mission.
Literature's aim, she said, is "to make us transparent to each other through what is
most opaque in the literary work."

Her discovery, as a girl, that she was "condemned to death," as she put it, led to a
preoccupation with death that informed much of Beauvoir's work. As she grew old,
however, death lost its power to intimidate her. "The idea of my end is with me; the
taste of the void is deep within me," she wrote in her final volume of memoirs. In her
last decades, writing remained her chief concern. While writing, she said, time seemed
to stand still.

Beauvoir died at the age of 78 from pneumonia. More than 5,000 people attended her
funeral. She is buried in Montparnasse cemetery, in the same grave with Jean-Paul
Sartre's ashes.

Eva Le Gallienne
January 11, 1899 - June 3, 1991

Eva Le Gallienne's father, the English poet Richard Le Gallienne, was a friend of Oscar Wilde's and knew Henrik Ibsen. Her mother, Danish journalist and feminist Julie Norregaard, had perched on Hans Christian Andersen's knee.

Her parents separated when she was four, and Eva was raised by her mother. By the time she was seven, she knew Paris, London, and Copenhagen, and read and spoke French, English, and Danish.

Her background prepared her to be a writer, but inspired by her mentors, Sarah Bernhardt and Eleonora Duse, Le Gallienne instead became one of the finest actors of the 20th century. Five-foot-four, slender, with fine-boned features, large, blue eyes, and a musical, cello voice, she dazzled audiences and critics with her consummate artistry.

Writing was in her blood, though, and since she spent most of her life as a working actor, her record of written work is extraordinary. Her translations of twelve of Ibsen's plays were published by Modern Library in two volumes. She wrote two autobiographies and best-selling translations of Hans Christian Andersen's stories, including *Seven Tales* (1959), *The Nightingale* (1965), and *The Little Mermaid* (1971). Her loving biography of Eleonora Duse, *The Mystic in the Theatre* (1966), is a classic.

In *Flossie and Bossie*, a moral fable for children of all ages (her only published work of fiction), Le Gallienne drew on her experiences with racial prejudice on her theater tours and the conflict between men and women and women and women. The inspiration for the story came one day when she was building a coop for "the poor little hen who has the one black chick ... The other hen with the five all-yellow treasures has turned out a perfect beast. She tries to peck the black chick all the time—and turns the poor little family out of one nest after another."

She named the rival hens Flossie and Bossie, and the chickens have all the foibles, pretensions, prejudices, and vanities of humans. A French lilac bush with pale mauve flowers, a shaded oak glade, a rose garden mulched with peat moss, and a predatory cat are images from the gardens and woods surrounding Le Gallienne's Weston, Connecticut, home.

Writing brought Le Gallienne serenity and self-awareness. Bossie philosophizes: "Humility and courage could go together then? You could be brave as well as meek? Long-suffering without the loss of kindness? For the first time Bossie felt less than perfect ... and the feeling ... filled her with a curious sense of peace."

Sunday
11

Eva Le Gallienne, b. 1899   Jack London, b. 1876   Alan Paton, b. 1903

 ## Monday
12

Tuesday
13

Horatio Alger, Jr., b. 1832

Wednesday
14

Yukio Mishima, b. 1925

Thursday
15

Molière, b. 1622

Friday
16

Saturday

Anne Brontë, b. 1820   Don Pedro Calderón de la Barca, b. 1600   17

January						
S	M	T	W	T	F	S
				1	2	3
4	5	6	7	8	9	10
11	12	13	14	15	16	17
18	19	20	21	22	23	24
25	26	27	28	29	30	31

January
1998

February						
S	M	T	W	T	F	S
1	2	3	4	5	6	7
8	9	10	11	12	13	14
15	16	17	18	19	20	21
22	23	24	25	26	27	28

+field @shu.edu

Sunday
18
A. A. Milne, b. 1882   Peter Mark Roget, b. 1779

Monday
19

Edgar Allan Poe, b. 1809
Martin Luther King, Jr. Day

Tuesday
20

Tutorial Seminars

Richard Le Gallienne, b. 1866

Wednesday
21
PDS Council - 3³⁰ OSC

6:00 reception - Holmes Group

Thursday
22

update critical path
documentation

George Gordon, Lord Byron, b. 1788

Friday
23

Saturday
24   Edith Wharton, b. 1862

January						
S	M	T	W	T	F	S
				1	2	3
4	5	6	7	8	9	10
11	12	13	14	15	16	17
18	19	20	21	22	23	24
25	26	27	28	29	30	31

January
1998

February						
S	M	T	W	T	F	S
1	2	3	4	5	6	7
8	9	10	11	12	13	14
15	16	17	18	19	20	21
22	23	24	25	26	27	28

Peter Mark Roget
January 18, 1779 - September 12, 1869

When he published the first edition of his
*Thesaurus of English Words and Phrases
Classified and Arranged so as to Facilitate
the Expression of Ideas and Assist in Literary
Composition*, Dr. Peter Mark Roget was 73
years old. He had been quietly at work on the
endeavor for nearly five decades.

A thin, clean-shaven man who habitually
wore black, Roget was better known as the
British doctor who had worked, free of
charge, for 18 years in a London charity
clinic and who had written and lectured on
scientific matters for most of his life. His
research interests ranged from animal

physiology, to phrenology, to water pollution, to motion pictures. He devised a slide
rule, tried to perfect a calculator, and designed a portable chess board.

His prose style was utilitarian rather than graceful. He had no training in etymology,
linguistics, or philology. He was not "literary." There was little, in fact, to suggest that
Peter Mark Roget was at all fascinated by words.

But he loved classifying things, organizing activity, presenting scientific data in an
orderly fashion. In compiling his "word book"—as he modestly called his thesaurus—
Roget aimed "to construct a systematic arrangement of ideas with a view to their
expression." He hoped the work would be useful to philosophers. Contrary to
expectation, the book found its most enthusiastic audience among editors, writers,
scholars, students, and devotees of crossword puzzles. (In 1925, the *New York Times*
proclaimed Roget the "Saint of Crosswordia.")

The word *thesaurus*, in Greek, means "treasury." For countless writers, Roget's book
has been just that. Neither a dictionary nor a simple listing of synonyms, Roget's
thesaurus presents fundamental concepts of human knowledge in such a way as to
reveal the "correlative" or "analogous" words which can best be used to express them.

His original, 100-page, penny edition thesaurus contained 1,000 concepts and some
15,000 words. By the mid-1980s, *Roget's International Thesaurus*—the only contemporary thesaurus officially derived from the original volume—included 256,000
words.

Roget continued adding words to his thesaurus until the day he died, at the age of 90.
He regarded his book less as a stylistic tool than as an instrument of truth. Language
must be specific, he advised. "A misapplied or misapprehended term is sufficient to
give rise to fierce and interminable disputes." In his pursuit of linguistic clarity, the
good Dr. Roget achieved his greatest legacy—and forever altered the way writers
write.

Richard Brautigan
January 30, 1935 - 1984

To young writer Keith Abbott, Richard
Brautigan looked like a "cross between Mark
Twain and a Heron." Compared often to
Twain and Hemingway, Brautigan had his
own distinctive, playful voice.

In *Trout Fishing in America* (1967), which
Brautigan wrote on a rickety card table while
on a camping trip through Idaho, the narrator
searches for the ideal trout stream. He finds
out that he can buy a used trout stream from
a wrecking yard in Cleveland for $6.50 a
foot. The nameless narrator of *In Watermelon
Sugar*, the best-selling novel of the hippie
generation, lives in a "shack near iDEATH"
and dips his pen in watermelonseed ink.

Brautigan lived in Haight-Ashbury in San Francisco during the 1960s. He wrote every
morning and then ambled around the city from bar to bar and friend to friend, often
playing word games and inventing puns and wacky metaphors. "Your alligator looks
like a handbag filled with harmonicas," says one of his characters.

Brautigan wrote without notes or an outline. He didn't keep a journal. "Whatever
happens to me," he said, "or any ideas I have sink back in the gunk until the time
comes to write ... I type very fast and I let the first draft come out as fast as it can."

Brautigan wrote quickly and prolifically. His books were read in England, France, and
Japan, but as he entered middle age and the times changed, his readership diminished.
According to his agent, Helen Brann, this "was breaking his heart."

In his last novel, *So the Wind Won't Blow it All Away* (1982), Brautigan drew on his
impoverished, traumatic childhood in the Pacific Northwest, where, he said, no one
ever believed that he would do anything good. Imagination saved him, and in his
work, he fashioned a "gentle carnival" which celebrated life's goodness and pleasure.
But, he wrote, "what makes you older is when your bones, muscles and blood wear
out, when the heart sinks into oblivion and all the houses you ever lived in are gone,"

In the early fall of 1984, he borrowed a .44 caliber Smith & Wesson, and went alone to
his house in Bolinas, California. On October 25, his badly decomposed body, with a
single gunshot wound to the head, was found.

Kurt Vonnegut, who knew Brautigan only through his writing, speculated that like so
many good writers, Brautigan "was finally done in by the chemical imbalance we call
depression, which does its deadly work regardless of what may really be going on in ...
the heartless marketplace."

Monday

26

mentors ey parents
check letters   *theater*

Lewis Carroll, b. 1832

 Wednesday

28

Dr. Cantini - 4:40 pm
mentors ey parents
                    7 pm

Sidonie-Gabrielle Colette, b. 1873

Thursday

29

TRU - 5:00 pm

Thomas Paine, b. 1737
Anton Chekhov, b. 1860
Eid-al-Fitr, Ramadan ends

Friday

30

Richard Brautigan, b. 1935

Saturday

Zane Grey, b. 1872   Freya Stark, b. 1893   31

January						
S	M	T	W	T	F	S
				1	2	3
4	5	6	7	8	9	10
11	12	13	14	15	16	17
18	19	20	21	22	23	24
25	26	27	28	29	30	31

January
1998

February						
S	M	T	W	T	F	S
1	2	3	4	5	6	7
8	9	10	11	12	13	14
15	16	17	18	19	20	21
22	23	24	25	26	27	28

Sunday

1

Monday

2

Ayn Rand, b. 1905   James Joyce, b. 1882

Tuesday

3

Gertrude Stein, b. 1874 *Steve /Orlando*

Wednesday

4

Thursday

5

Friday

6

Christopher Marlowe, b. 1564

Saturday

7   *Charles Dickens, b. 1812   Laura Ingalls Wilder, b. 1867*

February						
S	M	T	W	T	F	S
1	2	3	4	5	6	7
8	9	10	11	12	13	14
15	16	17	18	19	20	21
22	23	24	25	26	27	28

February
1998

March						
S	M	T	W	T	F	S
1	2	3	4	5	6	7
8	9	10	11	12	13	14
15	16	17	18	19	20	21
22	23	24	25	26	27	28
29	30	31				

James Joyce
February 2, 1882 - January 13, 1941

The English language had enough words for James Joyce, but they weren't the right ones. In *Finnegans Wake*, he replaced the days of the week with "moanday, tearsday, wailsday, thumpsday, frightday, shatterday." In *Ulysses*, he created vivid new adjectives such as "snotgreen sea. The scrotumtightening sea."

"Joyce had a spider's eye," observed his biographer Richard Ellmann. Plagued throughout his life by acute eye problems, Joyce struggled through pain, and a series of eye operations, to write the books on which his reputation rests—*A Portrait of the Artist as a Young Man*, *Ulysses*, and *Finnegans Wake*.

He estimated that he spent 20,000 hours writing *Ulysses*. He advised a writer friend not to plan ahead. "In the writing the good things will come," he said. Joyce wrote notes to himself on tiny bits of paper and stuffed them in his pocket. Later, he would decipher his miniscule handwriting with a magnifying glass. He kept a dream notebook and carefully recorded his own dreams as well as those of Nora, his wife. According to Ellmann, Joyce wrote best when he had the least time.

Born in Dublin on Groundhog Day into a large, Roman Catholic family, Joyce left Ireland (which he compared to an "old sow that eats her farrow"), and, using "silence, exile, and cunning," created a literary life for himself in Europe.

Joyce's unique vision was often misunderstood. Even his wife asked, "Why don't you write sensible books that people can understand?" D. H. Lawrence called his work "nothing but ... cabbage-stumps of quotations from the Bible and the rest, stewed in the juice of deliberate, journalistic dirty-mindedness." Hemingway disagreed. "Joyce has a most goddamn wonderful book," he enthused about *Ulysses*.

A novel that captured a single Dublin day (Thursday, June 16, 1904), *Ulysses* was banned as obscene, but the spirit of the book is pure joy. Joyce believed that his name, which derived from the French *joyeux* and the Latin *jocax,* was an omen.

Writing for Joyce was comparable to the mystery of the Mass. He wanted to "give people some kind of intellectual pleasure or spiritual enjoyment by converting the bread of everyday life into something that has a permanent artistic life of its own."

Anyone who has read through to Molly Bloom's ecstatic monologue at the end of *Ulysses* ("and first I put my arms around him yes and drew him down to me so he could feel my breasts all perfume yes and his heart was going like mad and yes I said yes I will Yes") knows that he succeeded.

Jules Verne
February 8, 1828 - March 24, 1905

After months of trying to sell his verse dramas, young Jules Verne realized that he lacked "contacts." He neglected his law studies at the Sorbonne and sought out the rich and famous. At one elegant dinner, he had the good fortune to knock Alexandre Dumas off his feet. The hugely successful author of *The Three Musketeers* and *The Count of Monte Cristo* brushed himself off, and later gave Jules some advice: "You must write, write, and write some more every day at a set time. ... If you keep writing, ideas will come to you."

Verne wrote, but his novels didn't sell. He had become fascinated with natural sciences, though, and he spent hours in the public library reading and making notes. The short scientific articles that he wrote were accepted quickly.

When Verne married a wealthy widow, he planned to devote himself to writing, but his father insisted that he take a position as a stock broker. Verne reluctantly complied and resigned himself to a boring, bourgeois life. A meeting with journalist and photographer Felix Nadar, who shared his enthusiasm about modern technology, changed his life.

Verne became caught up in Nadar's project to build a huge balloon and travel across Europe. The balloon was successfully launched, but the flight failed when the heavy balloon broke away from its lines and ripped apart. Verne was devastated. To counter his depression, he began to write. The result was his first book, *Five Weeks in a Balloon* (1863), which became a bestseller.

Other bestsellers followed, including *A Journey to the Center of the Earth* (1864), *From the Earth to the Moon* (1865), *Twenty Thousand Leagues Under the Sea* (1870), *The Tour of the World in Eighty Days* (1873), and *The Mysterious Island* (1875). Verne invented the genre of science fiction. His writing anticipated air conditioning, motion pictures, travel to the moon, the conquest of the poles, and atomic submarines. In fact, the first atomic submarine was christened the "Nautilus" in honor of Jules Verne's fictional creation.

In writing his 90 novels, Verne followed Dumas's advice. He wrote every day from 6:00 until noon. After lunch, he rested, then walked his dog. He worked in his library in the afternoon, making notes from his collection of scientific books. After 40 years of notetaking, his efforts resulted in over 20,000 pages.

He died before he saw the future that he had imagined so vividly. And the world mourned. A Paris newspaper announced, "The old storyteller is dead. Is it not as if Santa Claus had died?"

Sunday

8

Monday

9

Tuesday

10

 Wednesday

11

Thursday

12

parents/students -upper 4

Friday

13

Saturday

St. Valentine's Day   **14**

February						
S	M	T	W	T	F	S
1	2	3	4	5	6	7
8	9	10	11	12	13	14
15	16	17	18	19	20	21
22	23	24	25	26	27	28

February
1998

March						
S	M	T	W	T	F	S
1	2	3	4	5	6	7
8	9	10	11	12	13	14
15	16	17	18	19	20	21
22	23	24	25	26	27	28
29	30	31				

Sunday
15

Monday
16

Presidents' Day
Heritage Day (Canada)

Tuesday
17

Wednesday
18

Nikos Kazantzakis, b. 1883

Thursday
19

Carson McCullers, b. 1917

Friday
20

Saturday
21   *Anaïs Nin, b. 1903*

February						
S	M	T	W	T	F	S
1	2	3	4	5	6	7
8	9	10	11	12	13	14
15	16	17	18	19	20	21
22	23	24	25	26	27	28

February
1998

March						
S	M	T	W	T	F	S
1	2	3	4	5	6	7
8	9	10	11	12	13	14
15	16	17	18	19	20	21
22	23	24	25	26	27	28
29	30	31				

Nikos Kazantzakis
February 18, 1883 - October 26, 1957

The myth of Odysseus, Homer's wily hero, continues in the works of Sophocles, Seneca, Dante, Shakespeare, Racine, Giraudoux, Tennyson, and Joyce, and he lives vibrantly and completely in *The Odyssey, A Modern Sequel* by Nikos Kazantzakis. John Ciardi called the epic "a monument of the age."

Kazantzakis's masterpiece begins where Homer's ends. Odysseus leaves the bed of pale Penelope, sneaks like a thief from his home, and joins his companions on a new ship. "Forward!" he shouts. "Heave at the oars and make your minds a blank!" In 33,333 verses divided into 24 books, Kazantzakis chronicled the quest of Odysseus for freedom, for God, for the meaning of life itself.

Homer: the Source of Inspiration

It took 12 years for Kazantzakis to write his epic—"the efforts of an entire lifetime in the service of the spirit," he said. In all his writing, which included poems, plays, translations, and novels like *Zorba the Greek* and *The Last Temptation of Christ,* Kazantzakis had one vision of man. "What is our duty?" he asked. "To hold ourselves in front of the abyss with dignity. No tears, no laughter, to hide our fear. No closing of the eyes."

When he met Kazantzakis, his translator Kimon Friar felt that he was in the presence of a "lambent and transparent" greatness. A tall, elegant man with shaggy eyebrows and dark, olive-colored eyes, Kazantzakis was born in Crete. He earned a law degree from the University of Athens and studied with the philosopher Henri Bergson in Paris. A restless traveler, he knew five languages as well as Latin and ancient and modern Greek.

As protean as Odysseus, Kazantzakis never knew where his characters might lead him. When he sat down to write, he listened to the rhythm of his blood. "Both verse and emotion are created in a momentary flash," he said, "just as a man himself is created, body and soul, as one being." His lush prose is rich in metaphor and simile. In one gorgeous passage, he compares Odysseus's death to a flame that "leaps above its shriveled wick and mounts aloft, brimming with light, and soars toward death with dazzling joy, so did his fierce soul leap before it vanished into air."

With his wife, Helen, at his side, Kazantzakis died at 73 of leukemia in Freiberg, Germany. He is buried in the old Venetian Wall that surrounds the city of Herakleion in Crete.

Jane Bowles
February 22, 1917 - April 30, 1973

She was a "writer's writer's writer." Her collected works (one novel, one play, seven short stories) fit easily into one slim volume. A first edition of her only novel, *Two Serious Ladies* (1943), is a rare treasure. When it went out of print, even the author couldn't find a copy.

Jane Sydney Auer was born in New York. "When I was little I had to imagine that there was some limit to physical pain in order to enjoy the day," she remembered. A nurse dropped her when she was a baby; later she broke her leg falling from a horse, and then she developed tuberculosis of the knee, which left her with a limp. After two years in a sanatorium in

Jane and Paul Bowles in 1949

Leysin, Switzerland, Jane told her mother, "I am a writer, and I want to write."

She married the writer and composer Paul Bowles the day before her 21st birthday. They went to Panama on their honeymoon and spent most of their married life abroad, primarily in Tangier. At one time they lived with a cat, a duck, a parrot, a kitten, an armadillo, and two coatimundi. Tennessee Williams thought they were "a very odd and charming couple."

To Truman Capote, Jane Bowles seemed an "eternal urchin ... with some substance cooler than blood invading her veins, and with a wit, an eccentric wisdom no child, not the strangest wunderkind, ever possessed."

Living in Morocco stimulated Paul Bowles, but Jane felt "cut off from what I knew." She suffered from writer's block, and when she did write, she said it was like chiseling in granite. "I have done about thirty-three typewritten pages in the same number of days," she said. "One day I do three pages but then the next I do nothing ... and this is working all day and after dinner!"

Many of her characters are odd, eccentric women who live in exotic places. Her dialogue constantly surprises. In *Two Serious Ladies*, a man says, "There are people who live together and eat at table together stark naked all the year long ... but in my day ... we got what we paid for plus a dog jumpin' through burning hoops, and steaks you could rest your chin on."

Perhaps she wrote so sparingly because she lived so fully and so dramatically. Her own life, told in Millicent Dillon's biography *A Little Original Sin*, was filled with adventures and love affairs. Her last years, like her first years, were filled with unrelenting pain. After a long illness, she died in a Spanish convent near Tangier.

Sunday
22

Jane Bowles, b. 1917   *Edna St. Vincent Millay, b. 1892*   George Washington, born 1732

Monday
23

W.E.B. Du Bois, b. 1868   *Samuel Pepys, b. 1633*

Tuesday
24

Rosalía de Castro, b. 1837
Shrove Tuesday

Wednesday
25

Carlo Goldoni, b. 1707
Ash Wednesday

 ### Thursday
26

Victor Hugo, b. 1802

Friday
27

Henry Wadsworth Longfellow, b. 1807
John Steinbeck, b. 1902

Saturday
Michel de Montaigne, b. 1533   28

February						
S	M	T	W	T	F	S
1	2	3	4	5	6	7
8	9	10	11	12	13	14
15	16	17	18	19	20	21
22	23	24	25	26	27	28

February
1998

March						
S	M	T	W	T	F	S
1	2	3	4	5	6	7
8	9	10	11	12	13	14
15	16	17	18	19	20	21
22	23	24	25	26	27	28
29	30	31				

Sunday

1

Robert Lowell, b. 1917

Monday

2

Camille Desmoulins, b. 1760

Tuesday

3

Wednesday

4

2:00 - Celebration PDS Partnership

Thursday

5

Constance Fenimore Woolson, b. 1840

Friday

6

Elizabeth Barrett Browning, b. 1806
Ring Lardner, b. 1885

Saturday

7

March						
S	M	T	W	T	F	S
1	2	3	4	5	6	7
8	9	10	11	12	13	14
15	16	17	18	19	20	21
22	23	24	25	26	27	28
29	30	31				

March
1998

April						
S	M	T	W	T	F	S
			1	2	3	4
5	6	7	8	9	10	11
12	13	14	15	16	17	18
19	20	21	22	23	24	25
26	27	28	29	30		

Robert Lowell
March 1, 1917 - September 12, 1977

His favorite method of revision was to introduce a negative into a line of verse. Doing so reversed the meaning of the line, but often it also improved it. In a poem on Flaubert he changed the line "Till the mania for phrases dried his heart" to "Till the mania for phrases enlarged his heart." Lowell knew intuitively that the second line was superior to the first—even though the two signified opposite things.

He embraced ambivalence. He scorned his patrician Boston lineage but happily moved into a posh Boston house in 1955 and boasted of feeling "very lordly and pretentious" about it. Although fully one-third of the poems in his 1973 collection *For Lizzie and Harriet* dealt with Lowell's adulterous affairs, he dedicated the book to his wife and daughter.

Lowell inaugurated the notion of confessional verse. He began writing one of his best works, "91 Revere Street," a prose memoir of his father, on the advice of a psychiatrist. Lowell's manic depressive illness, his marriages, his loves, his neuroses all found their way into poems. "Is getting well ever an art, / or art a way to get well?" he asked.

Readers thrilled to the "shocking openness" of Lowell's 1959 *Life Studies*, "the most visible exemplum of the Confessional movement," remembers friend and fellow poet Richard Tillinghast. Lowell himself said of the book that its style marked "the biggest change in myself perhaps I ever made or will."

Always restless, ever seeking to reinvent himself, Lowell inspired in those who knew him a "sense of artistic perfectionism, of the necessity to live and breathe poetry," writes Tillinghast. "We asked to be obsessed with writing, / and we were," Lowell observed in the poem "For John Berryman."

Lowell's pleasure in writing was immense. He spoke reverently of the "blessed structures, plot and rhyme." He was passionate about language. He loved to ask other writers to name "the three greatest lines" of a given poet, or to invent a three-adjective description of some phenomenon. His own such descriptions were grounded in particulars: "neurasthenic, scarlet and wild," "diamond-pointed, athirst and Norman."

Of the dichotomy between pain and pleasure in his life, and the role these played in his work, Lowell said, "In truth I seem to have felt mostly the joys of living; in remembering, in recording, thanks to the gift of the Muse, it is the pain."

Fanny Trollope
March 10, 1779 - October 6, 1863

When her first book, *The Domestic Manners of the Americans*, appeared in 1832, Frances Trollope was 53 years old. The work, an idiosyncratic, unflattering portrait of the United States as seen by the British-born Trollope on her travels through America, sparked immediate controversy. Critics wondered how a woman could have written such a "vulgar" book. In New York, a wax effigy of Trollope went on display.

The Domestic Manners became an instant bestseller. Trollope used her earnings from the book to buy coal, candles, a "good bed and pillows," a sofa, and a chest of drawers. With future proceeds she hoped to purchase a cow and some malt for brewing.

She wrote the book to save her husband, herself, and their six children from financial ruin. For the next 25 years Trollope continued the practice, producing 40 books between 1832 and 1856, while at the same time fending off creditors, establishing and re-establishing the Trollope household (at one point the family moved six times in ten years), and tending to her ailing husband.

She began work punctually at four each morning and completed her quota of words before her family rose for the day. Her dedication was such that between 1834 and 1836, when she lost both her husband and two of her children to illness, Trollope wrote three books. While nursing her family she kept herself dosed with coffee in order to write. "The doctor's vials and the ink bottle held equal places in my mother's rooms," remembered her son Anthony, who as a novelist inherited his mother's disciplined habits.

In her travelogues and novels, Fanny Trollope tackled issues that others dodged: slavery, child labor, the inequality of women. She was, writes author Victoria Glendinning, "a true radical." She was caustic and sometimes crude. When her portrait was exhibited in 1833, one critic opined, "The painter has not flattered her good looks. He has had vinegar in his brush, too." At home, Trollope's children took to calling her "Madam Vinegar."

Throughout her career Fanny Trollope maintained a rigorous balance between her devotion to her family and her obligation to her craft. Upon her death in 1865, at age 84, *The Atheneum* called Trollope "one of the most remarkable women of her period. ... She wrote for bread, and reaped that honour. Her writings never bore the shadow of her circumstances. ... She had been tested as few women have."

Sunday
8

Monday
9

Vita Sackville-West, b. 1892

Tuesday
10

Fanny Trollope, b. 1779

Wednesday
11

 Thursday
12

Jack Kerouac, b. 1922
Gabriele D'Annunzio, b. 1863

Friday
13

Janet Flanner, b. 1892

Saturday
14

March						
S	M	T	W	T	F	S
1	2	3	4	5	6	7
8	9	10	11	12	13	14
15	16	17	18	19	20	21
22	23	24	25	26	27	28
29	30	31				

March
1998

April						
S	M	T	W	T	F	S
			1	2	3	4
5	6	7	8	9	10	11
12	13	14	15	16	17	18
19	20	21	22	23	24	25
26	27	28	29	30		

Sunday
15

Lady Gregory, b. 1852   Richard Ellmann, b. 1918

Monday
16

Tuesday
17

Kate Greenaway, b. 1846   Paul Green, b. 1894
St. Patrick's Day

Wednesday
18

Thursday
19

Friday
20

Ovid, b. 43 B.C.
Henrik Ibsen, b. 1828
Friedrich Hölderlin, b. 1770
Nikolai Gogol, b. 1809
Spring Equinox, 2:55 pm EST

Saturday
21

		March				
S	**M**	**T**	**W**	**T**	**F**	**S**
1	2	3	4	5	6	7
8	9	10	11	12	13	14
15	16	17	18	19	20	21
22	23	24	25	26	27	28
29	30	31				

March
1998

		April				
S	**M**	**T**	**W**	**T**	**F**	**S**
			1	2	3	4
5	6	7	8	9	10	11
12	13	14	15	16	17	18
19	20	21	22	23	24	25
26	27	28	29	30		

Paul Green
March 17, 1894 - May 4, 1981

Except for three years during World War II, every summer, for over half a century, Paul Green's outdoor drama, *The Lost Colony*, has thrilled audiences with its mixture of history, dance, and music. Staged at the Waterside Theatre on the shores of Roanoke Island on North Carolina's outer banks, the spectacle tells the story of 117 English men, women, and children who in 1587 sailed to the New World to establish a colony. Three years later, they had vanished without a trace.

Paul Green wrote 17 outdoor dramas, which he called "symphonic dramas." He believed that the Broad-way stage was too narrow and confined to "contain the richness of our tradition, folkways, singing, dancing and poetry." Green was also one of the first white American playwrights who wrote plays for black actors, but more important, says drama scholar Laurence Avery, "Green helped undermine racial stereotypes by treating black life honestly and realistically in his plays."

His drama *In Abraham's Bosom*, set in eastern North Carolina, tells the tragic story of Abraham McCranie, the son of a white man and a black woman. Produced by the Provincetown Theatre in 1926, the play won the Pulitzer Prize.

Born and raised in North Carolina, Green saw the South with an unsparing eye. In 1931, New York's Group Theatre chose his play about the decline of an old Southern family, *The House of Connelly*, as their first production, but they forced Green to change his tragic ending to a happy one. Green called the Group "yeasayers" who manipulated art for social ends. In the published version of his play, he used both the optimistic ending and the tragic ending.

Many of Green's plays were produced by the Carolina Playmakers at the University of North Carolina at Chapel Hill. His Broadway successes included *Roll Sweet Chariot* in 1934 (with a black cast), and an adaptation of Richard Wright's novel *Native Son*, which was directed by Orson Welles.

In addition to playwriting, Green wrote screenplays and taught philosophy and drama at the University of North Carolina. He was an early civil-rights activist, worked for UNESCO, and spoke out against the commercialization of the American theater.

Green wrote with realistic precision about ordinary people, but his writing is suffused with poetry. In his one-act play *Saturday Night*, an old farmer calculates that he has walked 75,000 miles behind a plow. "About as far as them stars," he says. "Wisht I'd done all my walking on a path going there."

Mary Webb
March 25, 1881 - October 8, 1927

She was 20 years old when Graves' Disease struck, rendering her an invalid unable to eat, drink, or sit up without help. The illness produced a goiter on her neck and made her eyes protrude. After six months in bed, where she nearly died, Mary Webb at last glimpsed herself in the mirror and was devastated.

Her convalescence lasted two years. During that time she often sat on the sofa in her parents' Shropshire home and stared at the soft blue hills in the distance. She loved the look and mood of Shropshire, which she called "the Border Country that merges into the Beyond." As a child she had learned from her father to pay attention to its most minute parts: bees, flower buds, clover, the effect of wind on a field of grass.

While she convalesced, Webb's father, and her childhood governess, Edith Lory, read to her from Shakespeare, the Bible, and her favorite poets. Eventually Lory suggested to Mary that she endeavor to record her thoughts and observations about nature. Tentatively, Webb embarked on a series of essays. In time these became *The Spring of Joy*, her first prose work. The collection heralds the curative power of nature and reveals Webb's discovery that between pain and spiritual gratification there is a curious bond.

"All that she wrote is suffused with poetry," said Walter de la Mare of Webb's work. G. K. Chesterton described the "light" in her stories as "a light not shining on things but through them." Between 1901 and her death in 1927, from Graves' Disease and pernicious anemia, Webb completed five novels and commenced a sixth. She also wrote poetry, having been tutored by her father in metrics, rhyme, and poetic form.

She labored over her books. She wrote with compulsive speed, scarcely sleeping, dropping sheets of script onto the floor in her haste to get to the next page. Typically her novels tell of disfigured heroines whose inner beauty inspires love. In Webb's own life, this was the case. At 28 she met and married schoolteacher Henry Webb, whose presence, she wrote in a dedication, "is home."

Although acclaimed in her time by her peers, Webb did not achieve widespread fame until shortly after her death, when Prime Minister Stanley Baldwin praised her work at a Royal Literary Fund Dinner, and in doing so established her name.

Mary Webb died at the age of 46. She is buried beneath a plain white cross in Shropshire, a land whose "magical atmosphere" endures through the grace and power of her work.

Sunday
22
Mothering Sunday (U.K.)

Monday
23

Fannie Merritt Farmer, b. 1857

Tuesday
24

Olive Schreiner, b. 1855

Wednesday
25

Mary Webb, b. 1881   *Flannery O'Connor, b. 1925*

Thursday
26

Robert Frost, b. 1874
Tennessee Williams, b. 1911

 Friday
27

Saturday
Maxim Gorky, b. (Gregorian calendar) 1928   28

March
S M T W T F S
1 2 3 4 5 6 7
8 9 10 11 12 13 14
15 16 17 18 19 20 21
22 23 24 25 26 27 28
29 30 31

March
1998

April
S M T W T F S
1 2 3 4
5 6 7 8 9 10 11
12 13 14 15 16 17 18
19 20 21 22 23 24 25
26 27 28 29 30

Sunday
29

Monday
30

Sean O'Casey, b. 1880

Tuesday
31

Andrew Marvell, b. 1621

Wednesday
1

Matsuo Bashō, b. 1644
Edmond Rostand, b. 1868

Thursday
2

H. C. Andersen, b. 1805
Giacomo Girolamo Casanova, b. 1725   *Clinical Issues PDS*

Friday
3   ↓

Washington Irving, b. 1783

Saturday
4   Marguerite Duras, b. 1914

March						
S	M	T	W	T	F	S
1	2	3	4	5	6	7
8	9	10	11	12	13	14
15	16	17	18	19	20	21
22	23	24	25	26	27	28
29	30	31				

March/April
1998

April						
S	M	T	W	T	F	S
			1	2	3	4
5	6	7	8	9	10	11
12	13	14	15	16	17	18
19	20	21	22	23	24	25
26	27	28	29	30		

Marguerite Duras
April 4, 1914 - March 3, 1996

"She writes, Marguerite Duras, yes,
M. D., she writes. She has pencils,
pens, and she writes. That's it.
That's all there is to it."

The words, spoken on French
television in 1988, belong to
Marguerite Duras, born Marguerite
Donnadieu in 1914 in the suffocat-
ing heat of French Indochina, where
her parents were teachers. As a child
Duras beheld unforgettable sights: a

boa constrictor devouring a chicken, diseased corpses waiting to be buried, a Vietnam-
ese worker falling from a ladder to his death. Of the last incident she said, "I knew
immediately that I had just discovered something tremendously important."

Inspired by her mother's stories of France, she wrote her first poems about snow. At
age 12 she announced, "I will write." At 18 she moved to France. In 1943 she
published her first novel, *Les Impudents*, under the pen name "Marguerite Duras."

Seven years later she brought out *The Sea Wall*, her "founding book," writes biographer Alain Vircondelet, "the one she [would] rewrite over and over." The book was
nominated for the Goncourt Prize but failed to win. The loss of this prestigious "boys'
prize," as Duras called the award, spurred her to greater achievement.

"My life is in the books," Duras remarked. "Not in order, but what does that matter?"
In her best-selling 1984 novel, *The Lover*, she recalled her clandestine adolescent
affair with a wealthy young Chinese man. In *The War* (1985), she evoked the terror of
wartime Paris and the torment of waiting for her husband to return from a German
concentration camp.

"When the past is recaptured by the imagination, breath is put back into life," Duras
said. She spoke of the "wonderful sorrow" of writing. It was the essence of her being.
At the height of her career she produced books at the rate of nearly one per year.
Writing was her "task." She wrote daily, as others "go to the office," she said.

Throughout her life Duras was consumed by the mysteries of love and sex, and she
wrote bluntly about both. She spent her last years in an unorthodox relationship with a
young homosexual man. As she struggled against illness in her final months, she
endeavored to keep a journal. Writing somehow sustained her. It "arrives like the
wind," she had observed years earlier. "... It is naked, mere ink, writing, and it passes
by like nothing else in life, nothing except life itself."

Thomas Hobbes
April 5, 1588 - December 9, 1679

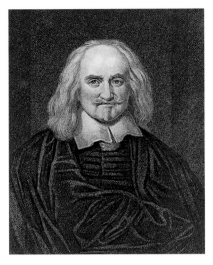

He was born in the town of Malmesbury, in Wiltshire, on Good Friday, in the year of the Spanish Armada. Rumors of an impending invasion were so rampant at the time that his mother, wrote Thomas Hobbes, "was big with such fear that she brought twins to birth, myself and fear at the same time." His kinship with fear, Hobbes added, taught him to loathe his country's enemies and to "ever serve Peace."

As a child he displayed a "yellowish" complexion and a "contemplative Melancholinesse," according to his first biographer, John Aubrey. Although "playsome enough," Hobbes was a serious, somewhat reclusive student who "would gett him into a corner, and learn his Lesson by heart presently." At Magdalen College, Oxford, where he attended school from the age of 14 to the age of 20, he studied logic and physics, reread the classics, and developed a passion for "maps celestial and maps terrestrial."

His curiosity about the world soon led Hobbes to the European continent, where he encountered such men as Galileo and the ideas of such men as Descartes. Hobbes returned to England ready, as he phrased it, "to be numbered among the philosophers."

He was 52 when he began to circulate his first major philosophical work, *The Elements of Law*, in manuscript form. The "small treatise," a compendium of advice on political conduct, revealed Hobbes's royalist bent. Fearing reprisal for his views, he took refuge in France.

His subsequent writings, notably *Leviathan*—in which Hobbes argues that human life, absent the body politic, is "solitary, poor, nasty, brutish, and short"—fueled debate on religious as well as political fronts. In his time, Hobbes pleased no person and no sect. He modelled himself on Don Quixote, whose "gallant Madness" he admired.

He lived to be 91. In later years he acquired a "fresh, ruddy complexion," and although he suffered from paralysis of the hands, he continued to write. At 89 he published a complete, metrical translation of the *Iliad* and the *Odyssey*. Asked why he had undertaken such a feat, Hobbes replied, "Because I had nothing else to do."

Convinced that "old men were drowned inwardly by their perspiration," Hobbes spent his final years walking up and down hills in an effort to rid himself of sweat. He sang out loud to improve his lungs, and he abstained from wine and red meat. Death nevertheless claimed him on December 9, 1679. It is said that Hobbes died "in all the forms of a very good Christian."

Sunday

5

Thomas Hobbes, b. 1588   Palm Sunday   Daylight Saving Time begins

Monday

6

Tuesday

7

William Wordsworth, b. 1770
Gabriela Mistral, b. 1889

Wednesday

8

Thursday

9

Friday

10

Clare Boothe Luce, b. 1903
Good Friday
Passover begins at sunset

 Saturday

11

April						
S	M	T	W	T	F	S
			1	2	3	4
5	6	7	8	9	10	11
12	13	14	15	16	17	18
19	20	21	22	23	24	25
26	27	28	29	30		

April
1998

May						
S	M	T	W	T	F	S
					1	2
3	4	5	6	7	8	9
10	11	12	13	14	15	16
17	18	19	20	21	22	23
24	25	26	27	28	29	30
31						

Sunday
12
Easter

Monday
13

Samuel Beckett, b. 1906
Nella Larsen, b. 1891
Easter Monday (Canada, U.K.)

Tuesday
14

Wednesday
15

Henry James, b. 1843

Thursday
16

Anatole France, b. 1844
J. M. Synge, b. 1871

Friday
17

Isak Dinesen, b. 1885
Thornton Wilder, b. 1897

Saturday
18

April						
S	M	T	W	T	F	S
			1	2	3	4
5	6	7	8	9	10	11
12	13	14	15	16	17	18
19	20	21	22	23	24	25
26	27	28	29	30		

April
1998

May						
S	M	T	W	T	F	S
					1	2
3	4	5	6	7	8	9
10	11	12	13	14	15	16
17	18	19	20	21	22	23
24	25	26	27	28	29	30
31						

The Alternative Press
April 12-18, 1998

On January 25, 1915, Virginia Woolf's 33rd birthday, Woolf and her husband resolved to buy three things: a house, a printing press, and a bull dog. Of the three items, Woolf was most excited about the press. As she was to learn, owning a press made her "free to write what I like."

VIRGINIA WOOLF

ORLANDO

THE HOGARTH PRESS

Vanessa Bell

Thirty years later Anaïs Nin described her dealings with the commercial press as a "subtle struggle against accepting money for compromising." Nin, like Woolf, turned to self-publication in order to preserve her integrity. She bought her own press and fell in love with the business of printing. Ink found its way into her hair, under her nails, inside the sandwiches she ate. She drew inspiration from the physical act of casting sentences in metal type. "The words which first appeared in my head, out of the air, take body. Each letter has a weight. I can weigh each word again, to see if it is the right one."

Fed up with the exigencies of commercial publishing, writers have long looked to the alternative press as an outlet for their work. The means are many: self-publication, small and university presses, little magazines, bookshop publishing, coffee house readings, *samizdat.*

Blake, Shelley, and Byron each at times relied on alternative publishing. Most major 19th-century American writers were self-published. Few 20th-century poets have found acceptance with the commercial press. Ezra Pound so detested commercial publishing—and the constraints it imposed on a writer—that he paid for the private publication of his poems. "So far as I personally am concerned the public can go to the devil," he said.

James Joyce's battles with both the commercial press and the censors are legendary. He himself paid to have *Dubliners* published; a small magazine issued *Portrait of the Artist as a Young Man* in serial form; and it was a bookseller, Sylvia Beach, who famously agreed to print, promote, and sell *Ulysses.*

But after 1922 Beach refused to publish any book other than Joyce's, so when Vladimir Nabokov asked in 1955 if she might publish *Lolita*—after five American houses had turned it down—Beach declined. The Paris-based Olympia Press brought out the novel instead. Known primarily for its editions of erotica, Olympia issued *Lolita*, like all of its offerings, in a titillating plain green cover. The book became a bestseller. Although Nabokov later disparaged Olympia's tawdry approach to his novel, he remained "deeply grateful" to the house. The alternative press had once more freed an author to write what he liked.

William Goyen
April 24, 1915 - August 30, 1983

"What starts you writing?" William Goyen
was asked. "It starts with trouble," he said.
"You don't think it starts with peace,
do you?"

He was born peacefully enough in Trinity,
a small town in East Texas. He grew up in
Houston, was educated at Rice University,
taught for a year, and during World War II,
he served on a navy aircraft carrier. After the
war, he moved to New Mexico, built a small
adobe house, and began to write. Frieda
Lawrence befriended him. "Frieda brought
me a sense of the richness of the great
world," Goyen remembered. "Here was a
woman who spoke of Goethe and Heine
and Moricke and read them to me."

Influenced by European writers, Goyen lived in Europe for a time, working on his first
novel, *The House of Breath*. Narrated by a boy in a small Texas town, the novel
captures the rhythms of his youth. "People in my life told me stories," Goyen said,
"and I sang. They had the speech, and I got the voice."

Goyen's voice is distinctive, lyrical, and theatrical. Anaïs Nin wrote that Goyen "has
given style to folk speech, elegance to colloquial expression." In an autobiographical
passage, Goyen speaks to his father: "hello Dad this is how I am, something marvel-
ous, to hell with your Texas yellow pine and cheap clothes and your poor low-down
family from the Mississippi sawmills, they won't break my heart anymore, why have I
cried for them in the night, a boy crying for a whole family, for the doomed generations."

Goyen was an evangelist of art, a true believer who felt that art and the holy spirit
were one. And yet his work is richly sensual. "Writing for me is totally physical," he
said. When he couldn't write, he waited. "If I push it ... I will find that I've overwrit-
ten it."

Although his *Collected Stories* was nominated for a Pulitzer Prize in 1975, and his
novels and stories were well-known in Europe, Goyen never enjoyed a wide popular
success in America. To augment his income, from 1966 to 1971 he worked as an
editor at McGraw-Hill, and he taught writing. Goyen enjoyed working with young
writers because he believed that everyone was a potential storyteller. Teaching, for
him, was helping writers to find their voice.

He didn't write for money or public acclaim, though. He cared most, he said, about the
"buried song in somebody, and sought it passionately."

Sunday
19

José Echegaray, b. 1832   Patriots' Day

Monday
20

Tuesday
21

Charlotte Brontë, b. 1816

Wednesday
22

Ellen Glasgow, b. 1873
Vladimir Nabokov, b. 1899
Madame de Staël, b. 1766
Secretaries' Day

Thursday
23

William Shakespeare, b. 1564
Bernard Malamud, b. 1914
Holocaust Remembrance Day

Friday
24

William Goyen, b. 1915
Anthony Trollope, b. 1815
National Arbor Day

Saturday
25

April						
S	M	T	W	T	F	S
			1	2	3	4
5	6	7	8	9	10	11
12	13	14	15	16	17	18
19	20	21	22	23	24	25
26	27	28	29	30		

April
1998

May						
S	M	T	W	T	F	S
					1	2
3	4	5	6	7	8	9
10	11	12	13	14	15	16
17	18	19	20	21	22	23
24	25	26	27	28	29	30
31						

Sunday
26
Anita Loos, b. 1888

Monday
27

Mary Wollstonecraft, b. 1759   Edward Gibbon, b. 1737
Muharram, Islamic year 1419 A.H.

Tuesday
28

Wednesday
29

Thursday
30

Friday
1

Saturday
2

			April			
S	M	T	W	T	F	S
			1	2	3	4
5	6	7	8	9	10	11
12	13	14	15	16	17	18
19	20	21	22	23	24	25
26	27	28	29	30		

April/May
1998

			May			
S	M	T	W	T	F	S
					1	2
3	4	5	6	7	8	9
10	11	12	13	14	15	16
17	18	19	20	21	22	23
24	25	26	27	28	29	30
31						

Anita Loos
April 26, 1888 - August 18, 1981

Every move she ever made, she said, was "motivated by s-e-x." In striving to be quotable, Anita Loos was not always accurate. Her long list of credits suggests that her motivation was w-o-r-k.

She began her career at two, modeling for her father's California newspaper. As a child actress, she played everything from "a snack for a man-eating lion" in *Quo Vadis*, to Little Lord Fauntleroy, to Nora's daughter in the American premiere of Ibsen's *A Doll's House*. At 13, she began her writing career, penning humorous anecdotes for the *New York Morning Telegraph*.

At 24, writing under the genderless name of "A. Loos," she sold her first silent film scenario, "The New York Hat," to *American Biograph* for $25. Mary Pickford played the winsome heroine who longed for a fashionable Easter hat, legendary D. W. Griffith directed, and the movie was a hit. It is still shown at the Museum of Modern Art in New York.

During her century-spanning career, Loos wrote four novels, three works of non-fiction, ten plays, five musicals, and some 155 screenplays, many of them forgotten, but she will always be remembered for *Gentlemen Prefer Blondes*. Loos said that she wrote the book "to make Henry Mencken laugh," which it did, with lines such as "a girl with brains ought to do something else with them besides think." She was the first American writer, Mencken said, "ever to make fun of sex."

Gentlemen Prefer Blondes, the story of sexy Lorelei Lee, the blonde gold digger from Little Rock, and her hilarious brunette sidekick, Dorothy Shaw, sold out immediately. Eighty-five editions followed. It has been translated into 14 languages, made into a play, two movies, and several musicals.

After she read it, Edith Wharton wrote Loos a postcard saying, "at last—the great American novel." William Faulkner lamented that he had not "thought of Dorothy first."

Under five feet tall, with round cartoon eyes, bobbed brown hair ("too much hair can smother a girl's ego," she said), and a fondness for Paris couture, Loos looked the part of the quintessential flapper. Her vast circle of friends was made up of Hollywood's elite stars as well as an intelligentsia that included Colette, Aldous Huxley, H. G. Wells, and astronomer Edwin Hubble. A Boston columnist once described her as "catnip for Harvard professors."

Loos spent her last years in Manhattan in an apartment on West 57th Street across from Carnegie Hall, attending so many parties, galas, events, and openings that the *New York Times* called her a "social institution." She died of a heart attack at 93.

May Sarton
May 3, 1912 - July 16, 1995

In the spring of 1937, May Sarton, then 25 and living in London, wrapped a copy of her first book of poems in tissue paper, bought a bunch of primroses, and walked to 52 Tavistock Square, the home of Virginia and Leonard Woolf. She presented her offerings to an old servant. A few days later, she received a note written in a "delicate spidery hand."

Later that spring, the poet Elizabeth Bowen introduced May to her idol. May thought Woolf looked like "some slightly unreal goddess ... the eyes set in the sculptured bone in such a way that their beauty was perfectly defined; her conversation was anything but ethereal."

Years later, after writing more than 50 books of fiction, poetry, and memoirs, May hoped that, like Virginia Woolf, she had presented her own unique vision of life, a "combination perhaps partly of my European background," she said, "plus the America I know and plus the temperament, the sort of passionate temperament, which is accompanied by a rather critical mind."

Her novels and her memoirs won her a loyal readership, but she was a poet first. "When it comes," she said, "it's like an angel." Although she wrote mostly in solitude, as a young woman she actively sought female mentors. "Women have been my muse," she said. At 17, stagestruck, she left her parents' home in Cambridge, Massachusetts, to join Eva Le Gallienne's Civic Repertory Theatre in New York. "My first great love was, in fact, the Civic Repertory Theatre," May remembered, "that kind of falling in love which frees the deep creative stream and forces one to grow."

To create her art, Sarton needed three hours of "primary intensity" a day. She wrote at her desk in the morning, the time when the "door to the subconscious is still open." After work, she walked her dog, rested, and in the afternoon, she read or gardened and went to bed early.

Through her writing and through her lectures, particularly on college campuses in the 1960s and 1970s, Sarton energized and gave courage to a generation of women. Her individuality and independence are vividly revealed in *May Sarton: Among the Usual Days*, a volume of poems, letters, journals, and photographs edited by Susan Sherman. The spirited artist and a contradictory image of her as a needy, lonely, and isolated woman emerge in *May Sarton*, Margot Peters's splendid biography.

May Sarton would not be surprised. In her novel *The Education of Harriet Hatfield*, she wrote, "One thing I am learning is that people are stranger and more mysterious than one can imagine."

Sunday
3

May Sarton, b. 1912   Mikhail Bulgakov, b. 1891   William Inge, b. 1913   Niccolò Machiavelli, b. 1469

Monday
4

May Day Holiday (U.K.)

Tuesday
5

Wednesday
6

Sigmund Freud, b. 1856

Thursday
7

Rabindranath Tagore, b. 1861
Edward Lear, b. 1812

Friday
8

Saturday

James M. Barrie, b. 1860   9

May						
S	M	T	W	T	F	S
					1	2
3	4	5	6	7	8	9
10	11	12	13	14	15	16
17	18	19	20	21	22	23
24	25	26	27	28	29	30
31						

May
1998

June						
S	M	T	W	T	F	S
	1	2	3	4	5	6
7	8	9	10	11	12	13
14	15	16	17	18	19	20
21	22	23	24	25	26	27
28	29	30				

Sunday
10
Mothers' Day   *Benito Pérez Galdós, b. 1843*

Monday
11

Mari Sandoz, b. 1896

Tuesday
12

Daphne du Maurier, b. 1907

Wednesday
13

Thursday
14

Dante Alighieri, b. 1265

Friday
15

Arthur Schnitzler, b. 1862
Katharine Anne Porter, b. 1890
L. Frank Baum, b. 1856

Saturday
16   Armed Forces Day

May						
S	M	T	W	T	F	S
					1	2
3	4	5	6	7	8	9
10	11	12	13	14	15	16
17	18	19	20	21	22	23
24	25	26	27	28	29	30
31						

May
1998

June						
S	M	T	W	T	F	S
	1	2	3	4	5	6
7	8	9	10	11	12	13
14	15	16	17	18	19	20
21	22	23	24	25	26	27
28	29	30				

Arthur Schnitzler
May 15, 1862 - October 21, 1931

"We know nothing of others, nothing of
ourselves," laments one of Schnitzler's
characters.

Arthur Schnitzler seemed to know everything about his characters. He diagnosed the
ills of fin-de-siècle Vienna in language that
combined grimy naturalism with lyric poetry.
Diagnosis came easily to Schnitzler, who,
like Chekhov, was a medical doctor as well
as a writer.

Born in Vienna, where he lived his entire
life, Schnitzler studied medicine at the
University of Vienna and became a
laryngologist. He had literary ambitions,
though, and joined a group of artists called Jung-Wien (Young Vienna), which
included the poet Hugo von Hoffmannsthal.

His first success as a writer came with *Anatol* (1893), a series of one-act plays that
follow the title character, "a hypochondriac in love," as he moves restlessly from one
woman to another. His play, *Reigen*, or *La Ronde* (1903), created a scandal. Schnitzler,
who was a Jew, suffered anti-Semitic attacks and was denounced as a pornographer.
An erotic round dance in ten scenes, *La Ronde* reveals how sexual relations cut across
all classes. For example, "The Prostitute and the Soldier" segues into "The Soldier and
the Parlormaid," which becomes "The Parlormaid and the Young Gentleman."

Schnitzler's probing insight into character and his interest in dreams and hypnosis
fascinated his contemporary Sigmund Freud. In a letter to Schnitzler, Freud confessed
that he had "tormented myself with the question why in all these years I have never
attempted to make your acquaintance ... I think I have avoided you from a kind of
reluctance to meet my double."

Scholar Larry Wolff calls Schnitzler the "doctor in attendance at the birth of the 20th
century." In his masterpiece, *The Road into the Open*, Schnitzler dissected Vienna's
cultured society, pondered how art and culture can exist when money and power seem
to have a higher value, and looked at a world in crisis that eerily foreshadows the end
of our own crisis-ridden century. The novel takes place in 1908, the year that Hitler
came to Vienna to study art. "Wherever I went, I began to see Jews," Hitler wrote in
Mein Kampf, "and the more I saw, the more sharply they became distinguished in my
eyes from the rest of humanity."

Schnitzler died in Vienna of a cerebral hemorrhage. "If you go to Vienna," says Larry
Wolff, "you can put a pebble on Schnitzler's grave site in the ravaged, untended
corner of the central cemetery where one portion of the population was buried apart."

Malcolm X
May 19, 1925 - February 21, 1965

Malcolm Little was an eighth grader in Mason, Michigan, when his English teacher urged him to begin thinking about a career. Thirteen-year-old Malcolm replied that he thought he'd like to be a lawyer. His teacher smiled. "Malcolm, one of life's first needs is for us to be realistic. Don't misunderstand me now. We all here like you, you know that. But you've got to be realistic about being a nigger. A lawyer—that's no realistic goal for a nigger." Years later, in his *Autobiography,* Malcolm X recalled, "The more I thought afterwards about what he said, the more uneasy it made me ... it was then that I began to change—inside."

He shunned all pretense of a "straight life" in his teens. He took up with a married white woman, became a ghetto hustler, and eventually landed in jail, where because of his "antireligious attitude," his fellow inmates nicknamed him "Satan."

"I'd put prison second to college as the best place for a man to go if he needs to do some thinking," Malcolm X later said. "If he's motivated, in prison he can change his life."

The prison library, and the inspirational example of a fellow inmate named Bimbi, allowed Malcolm Little to transform himself. He took a correspondence course in English, followed by one in Latin. He taught himself vocabulary by copying out the dictionary, page by page. He studied philosophy, religion, and, above all, history. He began telling other inmates about black history, and through prison debates—on topics as varied as compulsory military training, the Bible, and Shakespeare—he honed his oratorical skills.

After leaving prison, Malcolm Little joined the Nation of Islam and took a new name: Malcolm X. He gave his first, extemporaneous speech before a temple congregation in 1953. His remarks on Christianity and the horrors of slavery gripped listeners. He went on giving speeches, rousing crowds to embrace the cause of black liberation from white oppression. "My hobby," he said, "is stirring up Negroes."

His militancy antagonized many. By early 1965, Malcolm X knew he was a hunted man. On February 16, 1965, he told Alex Haley, to whom he had spent the previous two years dictating his *Autobiography*, that he was "marked for death in the next five days." On February 21, while giving a speech in Manhattan, Malcolm X was shot to death. At his funeral, actor Ossie Davis mourned the loss of "our own black shining Prince!—who didn't hesitate to die, because he loved us so."

Sunday
17
Dorothy Richardson, b. 1873

Monday
18

Victoria Day (Canada)

 Tuesday
19

Malcolm X, b. 1925
Lorraine Hansberry, b. 1930

Wednesday
20

Honoré Balzac, b. 1799

Thursday
21

Friday
22

graduation 2:00pm   *Arthur Conan Doyle, b. 1859*

Saturday
23

May						
S	M	T	W	T	F	S
					1	2
3	4	5	6	7	8	9
10	11	12	13	14	15	16
17	18	19	20	21	22	23
24	25	26	27	28	29	30
31						

May
1998

June						
S	M	T	W	T	F	S
	1	2	3	4	5	6
7	8	9	10	11	12	13
14	15	16	17	18	19	20
21	22	23	24	25	26	27
28	29	30				

Sunday
24

Monday
25

Ralph Waldo Emerson, b. 1803
Raymond Carver, b. 1938
Theodore Roethke, b. 1908
Memorial Day
Spring Holiday (U.K. ex. Scotland)

Tuesday
26

Wednesday
27

Rachel Carson, b. 1907
Dashiell Hammett, b. 1894
John Cheever, b. 1912

Thursday
28

Patrick White, b. 1912

Friday
29

Saturday
30   *Countee Cullen, b. 1903*

	May					
S	M	T	W	T	F	S
					1	2
3	4	5	6	7	8	9
10	11	12	13	14	15	16
17	18	19	20	21	22	23
24	25	26	27	28	29	30
31						

May
1998

	June					
S	M	T	W	T	F	S
	1	2	3	4	5	6
7	8	9	10	11	12	13
14	15	16	17	18	19	20
21	22	23	24	25	26	27
28	29	30				

Countee Cullen
May 30, 1903 - January 9, 1946

The circumstances of his birth are veiled in mystery. According to his second wife, Countee Cullen was born in Baltimore. According to Langston Hughes, his birth-place was Louisville, Kentucky. Cullen himself claimed he was born in New York City.

What is certain is that his mother abandoned him when he was a child. A woman named Elizabeth Lucas, who may have been his paternal grandmother, raised him until her death in 1918, at which point 15-year-old Countee Porter was unofficially adopted by the Reverend Frederick Asbury Cullen and his wife, of Salem Methodist Episcopal Church in Harlem.

Countee Cullen believed that a poet's life should not be open to inspection. Although popular, he was fundamentally shy. About the facts of his life, he was often secretive.

He described himself as "a rank conservative, loving the measured line and the skillful rhyme." His idol was John Keats. His first book of poems, *Color*, published in 1925, when Cullen was 22, established him as a brilliant star of the Harlem Renaissance. Langston Hughes proclaimed one of the book's poems, "Heritage," the most beautiful poem he knew.

Color remains Cullen's most enduring work. The poems in the volume are meticulously constructed in a range of traditional prosodic forms. Cullen insisted that poetry be "dignified," even "austere." He also insisted that black writers not dwell on the subject of race, for to do so would "strengthen the bitterness of our enemies."

He loved France and things French. In 1928 he spent a year in Paris on a Guggenheim grant. He found the city a liberation. "I have sought in you that alchemy / That knits my bones and turns me to the sun," he wrote in his poem "To France." "And found across a continent of foam / What was denied my hungry heart at home."

On his return to America, Cullen continued to publish poems, and one novel. But his work disappointed him. He spent his last years as a junior-high-school French teacher in New York City.

Paradoxically, it is for his poems about color that Cullen is most revered today. Small though his literary output was, Cullen performed a "fine and praiseworthy act," said W. E. B. Du Bois. By interpreting "his own subjectivity," Cullen revealed to the world the "inner workings" of the African-American soul and mind.

Thomas Mann
June 6, 1875 - August 12, 1955

Regardless of what befell him—illness, a death in the family, cataclysmic world events—Thomas Mann stuck to his schedule of three prose pages daily. When his son Klaus tried to commit suicide, Mann scolded him for having disturbed his serenity. When the young man tried again, and this time succeeded, Mann refused to interrupt a lecture tour in order to attend his son's funeral.

To the public, he projected an image of himself as a solid family man, devoted to his wife, Katia, and their six children. He built bourgeois homes and stocked them with servants. When he travelled he insisted on first-class accommodations. In his own words, Mann "administered" his fame, maintaining tight control over biographical accounts of his life and posing for photographs that showed him surrounded by an adoring family or the luminaries of his time.

He revered Goethe, and although he felt he never measured up to his idol, he sought to attain the man's enduring stature. "Goethe knew, and said," wrote Mann, "that it was only through the character and personality of the author that a work actually had influence and became a monument of culture."

In the 1890s, while working for a fire insurance company in Munich, Mann wrote short stories on the sly. He completed his first novel, *Buddenbrooks*, in three years' time. When his publisher demanded that he cut the huge book in half, Mann resisted. The unabridged, two-volume novel came out in 1901 and quickly became an international classic. Mann's fame was assured.

During the next 50 years, he produced a stream of novels that collectively define their age. *The Magic Mountain* (1924) probes the tensions that gripped society during World War I. *Doctor Faustus* (1947) exposes the sinister forces which allowed Nazism to prosper.

In *Death in Venice* (1912), Mann depicts an aging writer whose obsession with a beautiful young Venetian boy ultimately leads to the older man's death. The posthumous publication of Mann's diaries proved what many had suspected for years, that Thomas Mann shared with his protagonist, Gustav von Aschenbach, an erotic attraction to handsome young men.

Throughout his life, Katia Mann managed her husband's financial affairs, oversaw his social responsibilities, monitored his interviews, and kept his mornings free so that he could write. For Mann, life without Katia was unthinkable.

He won the Nobel Prize in 1929. Despite his claim that at best he enjoyed a "certain childlike intimacy with greatness," Thomas Mann remains a giant of 20th-century literature.

Sunday

31

Walt Whitman, b. 1819

 Monday

1

Holiday (Rep. of Ireland)

Tuesday

2

Thomas Hardy, b. 1840

Wednesday

3

Thursday

4

Friday

5

Federico García Lorca, b. 1898

Saturday

Thomas Mann, b. 1875   6

May						
S	M	T	W	T	F	S
					1	2
3	4	5	6	7	8	9
10	11	12	13	14	15	16
17	18	19	20	21	22	23
24	25	26	27	28	29	30
31						

May/June
1998

June						
S	M	T	W	T	F	S
	1	2	3	4	5	6
7	8	9	10	11	12	13
14	15	16	17	18	19	20
21	22	23	24	25	26	27
28	29	30				

Sunday
7
Elizabeth Bowen, b. 1889

Monday
8

Marguerite Yourcenar, b. 1903

Tuesday
9

Wednesday
10

Thursday
11

Ben Jonson, b. 1572

Friday
12

Anne Frank, b. 1929
Djuna Barnes, b. 1892

Saturday
13   *Fanny Burney, b. 1752   William Butler Yeats, b. 1865*

June						
S	M	T	W	T	F	S
	1	2	3	4	5	6
7	8	9	10	11	12	13
14	15	16	17	18	19	20
21	22	23	24	25	26	27
28	29	30				

June
1998

July						
S	M	T	W	T	F	S
			1	2	3	4
5	6	7	8	9	10	11
12	13	14	15	16	17	18
19	20	21	22	23	24	25
26	27	28	29	30	31	

Elizabeth Bowen
June 7, 1889 - February 22, 1973

As children, she and her cousin Audrey Fiennes made up stories about imaginary families. Between visits from Audrey, Elizabeth Bowen explored these fictive characters more deeply and shaped their lives into narratives of her own. It was her first foray into fiction.

She continued to tell stories as a student in Britain's Harpenden Hall. Together with a group of school friends, Bowen created dramas involving witchcraft and mysterious events. At the same time, she honed her powers of observation by studying art. Years later she remarked that "often when I write I am trying to make words do the work of line and color. I have the painter's sensitivity to light. Much (and perhaps the best) of my writing is verbal painting."

Critics compared her work favorably to that of Virginia Woolf, Henry James, E. M. Forster, and Jane Austen. Bowen's stories and novels convey complex truths about human relationships. Although frequently labelled a social realist, she is more accurately a literary impressionist. Much of Bowen's work stems directly from personal experience—her father's mental breakdown when she was a small girl, her mother's death from cancer, her childhood escapades with her cousin. Bowen once described her fiction as "transformed biography."

She was prolific. Between 1923, when she published her first volume of short stories, and 1975, when the final installment of her memoirs, *Pictures and Conversations*, appeared posthumously, she issued a new book almost every year. She also wrote reviews, essays, and articles for both British and American publications; travelled widely; and, as the wife of Alan Cameron, who served as secretary of education for the city of Oxford in the 1920s and later as an executive with the BBC, enjoyed an active social life.

During World War II, Bowen worked in London as an Air Raid Precautions warden. The war served as a backdrop to her novel *The Heat of the Day* (1949) and to a series of short stories. Critic Angus Wilson predicted, correctly, that in Bowen's war stories, future generations would find a striking portrait of London during this period of alternating violence and tenderness.

"Unlived lives," Bowen declared, gave her "the horrors." She thrived on setting and meeting goals for herself. She confessed once, famously, that what most frightened her was "a life to let." Towards the end of her life, in one of her last television interviews, Bowen was asked how she felt about aging. "I think the main thing," she replied, "is to keep the show on the road."

James Weldon Johnson
June 17, 1871 - June 26, 1938

On July 28, 1917, to the accompaniment of muffled drums, 10,000 black men, women, and children marched silently down Fifth Avenue in New York City. "Mr. President, Why Not Make America Safe for Democracy?" said one placard.

The Silent Protest March was organized by James Weldon Johnson, who was at the same time preparing his first volume of poetry, *Fifty Years and Other Poems* (1917), for publication. "I struggled constantly not to permit that part of me which was artist to become entirely submerged," he said.

Weldon was both artist and activist, and since he had "an abhorrence of spare time," his other occupations at various times included lawyer, journalist, diplomat, professor, anthologist, songwriter, novelist, school administrator, and teacher.

His early lessons were from his mother, who was the first black woman to work as a public school teacher in Florida. Since his school ended with the eighth grade, he continued his education through travel and reading. After spending a summer with his grandmother in New York amidst "rushing crowds," he realized that he was "born to be a New Yorker."

He continued his education in the south, graduating from Atlanta University, where he was prepared "to meet the tasks and exigencies of life as a Negro." One of his tasks was to compile three anthologies—*The Book of American Negro Poetry* (1922), *The Book of American Negro Spirituals* (1925), and *The Second Book of American Negro Spirituals* (1926). Johnson's finest work, however, was a volume of poems called *God's Trombones* (1927), which achieves universality and emotional power through soaring poetry that is based on old-time African-American sermons—an irony, since Johnson was an agnostic.

Johnson was an integrationist, and he looked to the future with optimism. As Ann Douglas points out in *Terrible Honesty*, her provocative book about Manhattan in the 1920s, Johnson believed that "American Negroes had equal claim to the privileges and opportunities of the country they helped to build ... [and] the same right, even at moments the same attraction, to the white artistic tradition as whites did to the black one."

In his autobiography, *Along This Way* (1933), Johnson warned that if whites did not share their power with blacks "there will be only one way of salvation for the race ... and that will be through the making of its isolation into a religion and the cultivation of a hard, keen relentless hatred for everything white."

Sunday

14

Harriet Beecher Stowe, b. 1811   Flag Day

Monday

15

Tuesday

16

 Wednesday

17

James Weldon Johnson, b. 1871   John Hersey, b. 1914

Thursday

18

Philip Barry, b. 1896

Friday

19

Blaise Pascal, b. 1623

Saturday

Lillian Hellman, b. 1905   20

| June |
S	M	T	W	T	F	S
	1	2	3	4	5	6
7	8	9	10	11	12	13
14	15	16	17	18	19	20
21	22	23	24	25	26	27
28	29	30				

June
1998

| July |
S	M	T	W	T	F	S
			1	2	3	4
5	6	7	8	9	10	11
12	13	14	15	16	17	18
19	20	21	22	23	24	25
26	27	28	29	30	31	

Sunday
21
Fathers' Day   Summer Solstice, 10:03 am EDT   *Mary McCarthy, b. 1912*

Monday
22

Erich Maria Remarque, b. 1898

Tuesday
23

Anna Akhmatova, b. 1889

Wednesday
24

Ambrose Bierce, b. 1842
St. John of the Cross, b. 1542

Thursday
25

Friday
26

Pearl Buck, b. 1892

Saturday
27   *Helen Keller, b. 1880*

June						
S	M	T	W	T	F	S
	1	2	3	4	5	6
7	8	9	10	11	12	13
14	15	16	17	18	19	20
21	22	23	24	25	26	27
28	29	30				

June
1998

July						
S	M	T	W	T	F	S
			1	2	3	4
5	6	7	8	9	10	11
12	13	14	15	16	17	18
19	20	21	22	23	24	25
26	27	28	29	30	31	

Ambrose Bierce
June 24, 1842 - 1914 (?)

While his contemporaries Henry James, William Dean Howells, and Samuel Clemens all found ways to avoid serving in the Civil War, Ambrose Bierce soldiered with the Ninth Indiana and fought at Shiloh, Stones River, and Chickamauga.

Wounded by a musket ball to the head, Bierce recovered from his injury, but he never recovered from the horrors he had witnessed. In "One Officer, One Man," he noted that the blood had a "faint, sweetish odor that sickened him. The face was crushed into the earth and flattened. It looked yellow already, and was repulsive. Nothing suggested the glory of a soldier's death ..."

His classic stories "Chickamauga" and "An Occurrence at Owl Creek Bridge," and the nonfiction "What I Saw at Shiloh," showed the way for Stephen Crane, Ernest Hemingway, Norman Mailer, and Tim O'Brien. Bierce's writing is "the working prototype of all modern war literature," asserts Roy Morris, Jr., in his biography of Bierce.

The Civil War changed Bierce, turning him into a man, who, according to Jack London, would "bury his best friend with a sigh of relief, and express satisfaction that he was done with him."

"Bitter Bierce," as he came to be called, was born in Horse Cave Creek, Ohio, into a family of nine children, all with names beginning with the letter "A." His father had a fine library, and Bierce said, "All that I have I owe to his books."

Perhaps books and writing were the only true loves of Bierce's life. He had an unhappy marriage and was estranged from his three children. In addition to his stories and tales, he worked as a journalist in San Francisco, England, and later in Washington, D.C. His literary criticism was likened to "breaking butterflies on a wheel," and the misanthropic Bierce attacked everyone indiscriminately. He defined religion as "a daughter of Hope and Fear, explaining to Ignorance the Unknowable." He signed his columns simply "AG"—which stood for Almighty God, quipped one wag.

In 1911, he published *The Devil's Dictionary*, a black comic compilation of ironic definitions. "ALONE, adj. In bad company" could serve as his epitaph. In December 1913 Bierce vanished. Legend holds that he went to Mexico to serve with Pancho Villa and was killed there. Roy Morris, Jr., makes a strong case for Bierce's taking his own life.

His fate is unknowable, which is fitting for a man who defined history as "an account mostly false, of events mostly unimportant, which are brought about by rulers mostly knaves, and soldiers mostly fools."

Charlotte Perkins Gilman
July 3, 1860 - August 17, 1935

"Twenty-one. My own mistress at last," wrote Charlotte Perkins. "No one on earth had a right to ask obedience of me."

Descended from the Beecher family of New England, part of a long line of freethinkers, radicals, and writers, Charlotte was raised by her mother (her father left when she was quite young). Largely self-taught, she read widely in philosophy, literature, and feminism, learned French and German, and wrote poems and stories. At 21, she prided herself on being self-supporting.

A few years later, she married Walter Stetson. In 1885, she gave birth to a baby girl and became so severely depressed that she could not work. She sought treatment for "neurasthenia." Her doctor prescribed a regimen which was currently popular: "Live as domestic a life as possible ... And never touch pen, brush, or pencil as long as you live."

Charlotte followed his advice for months and came, she said, "perilously near to losing my mind."

Instead of losing her mind, she separated from her husband, sent her daughter to live with Stetson and his new wife, and began to work again, writing and lecturing, even running a boardinghouse. (In 1900, she married her cousin, G. Houghton Gilman.)

And, she turned her agony into art. In 1892, she wrote the classic story "The Yellow Wallpaper." The harrowing, first-person study of a woman's descent into madness has been widely anthologized, and playwright Constance Congdon wrote an opera based on it. Gilman had written the story to save herself, but she also sent the story to her doctor, and he changed his treatment, which undoubtedly saved countless others.

Work gave her pleasure and power. One day she wrote 4,000 words in a "smooth, swift, easy flow" and was so overcome with joy that she "went and ran, just raced along the country road, for sheer triumph."

She devoted most of her life to her socialist and feminist ideals. Her book *Women and Economics* (1898) won her an international reputation and was translated into seven languages, and in 1915 she published *Herland*, her famous utopian novel, which imagined a perfect all-female world. George Bernard Shaw and H. G. Wells admired her intellect, and Rebecca West called her "the greatest woman in the world today."

"There is no female mind," Charlotte asserted, as if challenging West's category. "The brain is not an organ of sex. As well speak of a female liver."

Sunday

28

Luigi Pirandello, b. 1867

Monday

29

Antoine de Saint-Exupéry, b. 1900

Tuesday

30

 Wednesday

1

George Sand, b. 1804
Susan Glaspell, b. 1873
Canada Day

Thursday

2

Friday

3

Charlotte Perkins Gilman, b. 1860   *Franz Kafka, b. 1883*

Saturday

Nathaniel Hawthorne, b. 1804   Declaration of Independence, 1776   4

June						
S	M	T	W	T	F	S
	1	2	3	4	5	6
7	8	9	10	11	12	13
14	15	16	17	18	19	20
21	22	23	24	25	26	27
28	29	30				

June/July
1998

July						
S	M	T	W	T	F	S
			1	2	3	4
5	6	7	8	9	10	11
12	13	14	15	16	17	18
19	20	21	22	23	24	25
26	27	28	29	30	31	

Sunday

5

Jean Cocteau, b. 1889

Monday

6

Mawlid, Prophet Mohammed born c. 570

Tuesday

7

Robert A. Heinlein, b. 1907

Wednesday

8

Thursday

9

Friday

10

Saturday

11   *E. B. White, b. 1899*

July						
S	M	T	W	T	F	S
			1	2	3	4
5	6	7	8	9	10	11
12	13	14	15	16	17	18
19	20	21	22	23	24	25
26	27	28	29	30	31	

July
1998

August						
S	M	T	W	T	F	S
						1
2	3	4	5	6	7	8
9	10	11	12	13	14	15
16	17	18	19	20	21	22
23	24	25	26	27	28	29
30	31					

On the Move

Some writers never travel. Their rambles are all in the imagination. Think of Emily Brontë striding with her dogs across the Yorkshire moors, or Flannery O'Connor surrounded by her peacocks on her Georgia farm. For most of his life, Flaubert sat at the same desk in the same room in his Rouen suburb, sculpting sentences. Every day Wallace Stevens walked the same path to his office, composing poems to the rhythm of his breathing.

For others, breathing the air in a foreign setting, seeing strange people, and listening to unfamiliar languages releases creativity and awakens impulses that might not have been realized in the safe, sometimes stale atmosphere of home.

After seven years in prison, Breyten Breytenbach arrives in France with his wife, Yolande, in 1982.

Their journeys to fabled places prompted medieval pilgrims to produce the world's first travel guides and Columbus and his fellow explorers to forge a new literary genre: the travel memoir. Subsequent generations turned the form into high art. Countless armchair travellers have accompanied the likes of Robert Louis Stevenson, Herman Melville, Henry James, and Bruce Chatwin on memorable expeditions to exotic lands.

Others have made travel the source—rather than the subject—of their work. Ibsen wrote his finest plays, *Peer Gynt*, *A Doll's House*, *Ghosts*, and *Hedda Gabler*, not in his native Norway, but in Italy and Germany. An entire generation of Americans, including Ernest Hemingway, Gertrude Stein, Djuna Barnes, T. S. Eliot, and Ezra Pound, fled to Paris in the 1920s to find a climate receptive to their art.

James Baldwin left America and settled in France—but he never forgot his birthplace, and in book after book he wrote about his youth in Harlem. Exiled from South Africa, Breyten Breytenbach found it impossible to forget his homeland. "Wherever a man goes, he takes his house with him," Breytenbach has written.

Vita Sackville-West believed that "travel is the most private of pleasures." When life became too oppressive for Tennessee Williams, he would cry "En avant!" and jump on a plane. For Laurence Sterne, travel was as capricious an undertaking as writing itself. "I think there is a fatality in it," he said of his wanderings. "I seldom go to the place I set out for."

"Travellers, poets, and liars are three words all of one signification," declared the 17th-century writer Richard Brathwaite. The 20th-century Mallorcan author Lorená Villalonga was more explicit. "Travelling and writing," he states in one of his novels, "are the same thing."

Natalia Ginzburg
July 14, 1916 - October 7, 1991

Growing up, Natalia Ginzburg was the "little sister" in her family. When one is the youngest, she said later, "people are always telling you to hurry up, get to the point, say what you mean. I think that's why I write the way I do."

And she wrote simply. "No virtuoso turns occlude the lens through which she sees the world; nothing of the merely literary clogs the narrative," observes American novelist Mary Gordon, who first stumbled upon Ginzburg's work in an Italian bookstore in 1971 and became an avid fan.

Because she wrote about such things as families and the interior lives of women and children, Ginzburg has often been classified as a minor writer. Even she remarked that when she wrote something, she generally thought it "very important. ... But there is one corner of my mind in which I know very well what I am, which is a small, a very small writer." And yet: "I write about families because that is where everything starts."

Born in Palermo and raised in Turin, Ginzburg began writing verse as a girl. Poetry led to prose. She struggled to emulate Chekhov. At 17 she composed what she called her "first real story," written during a single setting on a summer evening. The effort taught her that she could write "millions of stories."

In 1938 she married Leone Ginzburg, a Jewish Marxist from Turin. Two years later the Fascist government deported the couple and their two children to an impoverished village in southern Italy. During their confinement, Natalia gave birth to a third child. Despite the burden of exile and the demands of motherhood, she managed to complete her first novel. She later said that although she did not know it then, these years were "the best time of my life."

Following Mussolini's death in 1943, German forces occupied Italy. Leone Ginzburg was arrested and tortured. He died in jail. Natalia and her children went into hiding under assumed, non-Jewish names. After the war, a semblance of normalcy returned. Ginzburg took a job with a publishing house, resumed writing, and eventually remarried. In the next three decades she produced a half-dozen works of essays, stories, memoirs, a literary biography, and a play. Her writing invariably sprang from personal experience. "I cannot in any way invent things out of thin air."

Asked once to describe how the events of her life had shaped her work, Ginzburg answered, "I think of a writer as a river: you reflect what passes before you."

Sunday

12

Madame Blavatsky, b. 1831   Pablo Neruda, b. 1904   Henry D. Thoreau, b. 1817   Johanna Spyri, b. 1827

Monday

13

Holiday (N. Ireland)

Tuesday

14

Natalia Ginzburg, b. 1916
F. R. Leavis, b. 1895
Isaac Bashevis Singer, b. 1904

Wednesday

15

 Thursday

16

Friday

17

Saturday

William Makepeace Thackeray, b. 1811   **18**

July						
S	M	T	W	T	F	S
			1	2	3	4
5	6	7	8	9	10	11
12	13	14	15	16	17	18
19	20	21	22	23	24	25
26	27	28	29	30	31	

July
1998

August						
S	M	T	W	T	F	S
						1
2	3	4	5	6	7	8
9	10	11	12	13	14	15
16	17	18	19	20	21	22
23	24	25	26	27	28	29
30	31					

Sunday
19

Monday
20

Petrarch, b. 1304

Tuesday
21

Hart Crane, b. 1899
John Gardner, b. 1933
Ernest Hemingway, b. 1899

Wednesday
22

Emma Lazarus, b. 1849

Thursday
23

Friday
24

Alexandre Dumas, père, b. 1802

Saturday
25

July						
S	M	T	W	T	F	S
			1	2	3	4
5	6	7	8	9	10	11
12	13	14	15	16	17	18
19	20	21	22	23	24	25
26	27	28	29	30	31	

July
1998

August						
S	M	T	W	T	F	S
						1
2	3	4	5	6	7	8
9	10	11	12	13	14	15
16	17	18	19	20	21	22
23	24	25	26	27	28	29
30	31					

Emma Lazarus
July 22, 1849 - November 19, 1887

When Emma Lazarus was first asked to write a dedicatory poem for Frederic-Auguste Bartholdi's statue called "Liberty Enlightening the World," she refused. She was busy working on the cause of Jews who had fled persecution in Russia and resettled in New York. When a friend reminded her that the statue might mean a great deal to immigrants fleeing oppression, Lazarus agreed to take on the job. When she wrote the poem, the 151-foot statue was still in Paris. Lazarus called her sonnet "The New Colossus." For her, writing the poem was a political act.

In her poem, the statue speaks, a "mighty woman with a torch." "Give me your tired, your poor, / Your huddled masses yearning to breathe free, / The wretched refuse of your teeming shore. / Send these, the homeless, tempest-tost to me, / I lift my lamp beside the golden door!"

To Emma Lazarus, America was a golden place. The daughter of a wealthy Jewish industrialist, she grew up privileged and protected and enjoyed all the benefits of New York City's culture and fashionable society. Too frail to attend school, she was educated at home by tutors. "Books were her world from her earliest years," recalled her sister. "In them she literally lost and found herself."

Her first book, *Poems and Translation* (1867), was published when she was just 18. In addition to her own poems, she also included translations of poems by Hugo, Dumas, Schiller, and Heine, demonstrating a remarkable facility with English, French, and German.

In her early 20s, she began a correspondence with 65-year-old Ralph Waldo Emerson, who encouraged her work. She dedicated her second book, *Admetus, and Other Poems* (1871), to him. Turgenev praised her novel *Alide* (1874), which was inspired by Goethe's life. The Russian pogroms in the early 1880s stimulated her interest in refugees. In *Songs of a Semite* (1882), she wrote poems and translated Hebrew poets in an effort to gain support for her people. In her essays, she also was one of the first to call for the formation of a Jewish state.

During her short life, Lazarus supported Jewish and humanitarian causes, and she enjoyed popular acclaim as a widely read poet and essayist. Today, however, she's remembered for "The New Colossus," written when she was 34. In the last few years of her life, she suffered from Hodgkins disease, but she managed to produce *By the Waters of Babylon* (1887), a volume of prose poems. She died at 38.

Summary

Anaïs Nin compared the softness of a summer day to "an ermine paw."

Christina Rossetti pronounced winter "cold-hearted," spring "yea and nay," and autumn a "weather-cock." "Summer days for me," she wrote, "When every leaf is on its tree."

It's a season for fishing and baseball, ice cream and outdoor concerts, picnics on the beach and idle afternoons reading books in a hammock. It's a time for shedding routines as well as clothes, for doing nothing. It's a land "of freedom felt in the body itself," suggests John Updike.

Ernest Hemingway spent his childhood summers by the water, fishing, sailing, hunting, and hiking with his family during their yearly visit to the north Michigan woods. Years later, in his "Nick Adams" stories, Hemingway transformed those summers into fiction.

For those who stay at home—"that is, most of the world," Elizabeth Hardwick reminds us—summer has its own domestic patterns. The furnace is shut down and windows raised. There's the drone of the lawn mower and a profusion of color in the garden. "The congratulation of summer is that it can make the homely and the humble if not exactly beautiful, beautifully acceptable," writes Hardwick.

It's a time for romance. Edith Wharton puts a love affair at the heart of her short novel *Summer*. Tess and Angel Clare fall in love against a ripening summer landscape in Hardy's *Tess of the D'Urbervilles*. Summer's light wreaks amatory havoc in Shakespeare's *A Midsummer Night's Dream*.

For Anatole Broyard, summer "was an ambiguous space that I had to fill with decision. Summer was my first attempt to entertain myself, to manage my own life, to plan."

For Federico García Lorca, summer was an occasion for writing. Unable to resist the distractions of social life during the winter, he found in the quiet of his father's summer home in Andalusia the seclusion and repose he needed in order to create.

In the first stanza of "Summer Serenade," Ogden Nash captures the essence of the season: "When the thunder stalks the sky, / When ticklefooted walks the fly, / When shirt is wet and throat is dry, / Look, my darling, that's July."

And, all too soon, summer fades. "How softly summer shuts," observes Emily Dickinson, "without the creaking of a door."

Sunday

26

George Bernard Shaw, b. 1856   *Antonio Machado, b. 1875*

Monday

27

Tuesday

28

Beatrix Potter, b. 1866
Gerard Manley Hopkins, b. 1844

Wednesday

29

Booth Tarkington, b. 1869

Thursday

30

Giorgio Vasari, b. 1511
Emily Brontë, b. 1818

 Friday

31

Saturday

Herman Melville, b. 1819   1

July						
S	M	T	W	T	F	S
			1	2	3	4
5	6	7	8	9	10	11
12	13	14	15	16	17	18
19	20	21	22	23	24	25
26	27	28	29	30	31	

July/August
1998

August						
S	M	T	W	T	F	S
						1
2	3	4	5	6	7	8
9	10	11	12	13	14	15
16	17	18	19	20	21	22
23	24	25	26	27	28	29
30	31					

Sunday

2

James Baldwin, b. 1924

Monday

3

Holiday (Rep. of Ireland)

Tuesday

4

W.H. Hudson, b. 1841
Knut Hamsun, b. 1859

Wednesday

5

Thursday

6

Alfred Lord Tennyson, b. 1809

Friday

7

Alice James, b. 1848

Saturday

8   *Marjorie Kinnan Rawlings, b. 1896   Sara Teasdale, b. 1884*

August						
S	M	T	W	T	F	S
						1
2	3	4	5	6	7	8
9	10	11	12	13	14	15
16	17	18	19	20	21	22
23	24	25	26	27	28	29
30	31					

August
1998

September						
S	M	T	W	T	F	S
		1	2	3	4	5
6	7	8	9	10	11	12
13	14	15	16	17	18	19
20	21	22	23	24	25	26
27	28	29	30			

W. H. Hudson
August 4, 1841 - August 18, 1922

By the time he was six, W. H. Hudson could ride a horse bareback at a gallop across the broad Argentine plain known as the pampas. He was born on a ranch in the pampas, near Buenos Aires, the son of immigrants from New England and the grandson of a Devonshire farmer.

His boyhood in Argentina shaped the eventual course of Hudson's life and work. He revelled in the variety and activity of natural life to be found on the pampas. Above all, he loved its birds—migratory birds from both the subtropics and Patagonia and Antarctica, who fed on the vast Argentine plain. Hudson became an expert on the subject of birds, and in his mid-20s was commissioned by the Smithsonian Institute to collect bird skins, a practice he later repudiated when it included endangered species.

His first published work was a series of letters on South American birds, written to and for the Zoological Society of London, who printed the correspondence in its *Proceedings*. Emboldened by this event, Hudson impulsively set sail for England in 1874, at age 28. He never returned to Argentina.

In London, he embarked on a romantic novel about an English family living in South America. Eventually he published a section of the book, but he destroyed the rest of the manuscript. Later, Hudson pronounced himself weak in narrative skills.

His genius was nature writing. His observations on nature possess not only literary but scientific merit. In his letters to the Zoological Society, Hudson challenged Darwin— and received a conciliatory letter from the naturalist on the matter of a specific South American woodpecker. In 1892, Hudson achieved his first unqualified success with *The Naturalist in La Plata*. He followed this with such works as *Idle Days in Patagonia*, a memoir of his youth in Argentina, and several works on British birds. He also wrote novels, most notably *Green Mansions: A Romance of the Tropical Forest* (1904).

In what is perhaps his most enduring work, *A Shepherd's Life* (1910), Hudson recalls his conversations with a Wiltshire shepherd whom he first met in 1901. Hudson never questioned the man directly, but instead drew him out by recounting the sights and sounds he himself had experienced during his wanderings through the British countryside.

Late in life, W. H. Hudson authorized the republication of his earliest books so as to increase the value of his estate. At his death, he left everything to the Society for the Preservation of Birds.

Louise Colet
August 15, 1810 - March 8, 1876

Her face cast a spell on nearly everyone she encountered. "The flaxen radiance of her blond hair, which fell unto each temple in cascades of curls, had golden gleams, which recalled the dazzling halos of saints," wrote one of Louise Colet's contemporaries.

In the journal she began at the age of 34 and kept, sporadically, through the most turbulent years of her life, Colet wrote of her beauty: "My throat, my shoulders, my arms, are exceptionally lovely. My neck is still admired for the manner in which it is joined to my head, but that is actually a defect because it causes my face to appear too round."

She came to Paris in 1835, the wife of a provincial musician, and within three years won a prestigious poetry competition sponsored by the Académie Française. Months later she became the lover of the Académie's most famous constituent, Victor Cousin. She established her own salon, befriended the city's elite, produced her first play—*Goethe's Youth*—and left her husband. In 1840 she gave birth to a daughter, Henriette, who was apparently Cousin's child.

Louise Colet met Gustave Flaubert in 1846. Soon afterward the two became lovers. Their letters to one another comprise one of literature's most rapturous epistolary exchanges. "Your little slippers are here even as I write, facing me, I stare at them," wrote Flaubert, twelve hours after leaving Colet's bed for the first time. "... The handkerchief is also with them, I see your blood—I wish it were drenched with it."

In time the affair ran its course. But for both Colet and Flaubert it remained the most passionate liaison of their lives. Eventually, Louise Colet became Flaubert's principal inspiration while writing *Madame Bovary*.

As writers, the two were opposites. Flaubert regarded writing as a sacred calling. Colet viewed it as a means of attaining both "glory" and a living wage with which to support herself and her daughter. Her poetry—which Flaubert disparaged as "totally false in sentiment and expression"—continued to win prizes from the French Academy.

She never gave up writing. In the last year of her life, at age 65, her legendary beauty long gone, Colet labored to complete a prose volume on the Orient and a new collection of verse. "Even if it kills me, I must finish," she told her secretary. At her death, Flaubert mourned the loss of "my poor Muse," as he phrased it. "Ah!" he confided to a friend. "Misery on us all!"

Sunday
9

Monday
10

Tuesday
11

Louise Bogan, b. 1897

Wednesday
12

Edith Hamilton, b. 1867
Mary Roberts Rinehart, b. 1876

Thursday
13

 Friday
14

Saturday

Edna Ferber, b. 1855   *Sir Walter Scott, b. 1771*   *Louise Colet, b. 1810*
Thomas De Quincey, b. 1785   15

August						
S	M	T	W	T	F	S
						1
2	3	4	5	6	7	8
9	10	11	12	13	14	15
16	17	18	19	20	21	22
23	24	25	26	27	28	29
30	31					

August
1998

September						
S	M	T	W	T	F	S
		1	2	3	4	5
6	7	8	9	10	11	12
13	14	15	16	17	18	19
20	21	22	23	24	25	26
27	28	29	30			

Sunday
16

Monday
17

Tuesday
18

Elsa Morante, b. 1918

Wednesday
19

Ogden Nash, b. 1902

Thursday
20

H.P. Lovecraft, b. 1890

Friday
21

Saturday
22   *Dorothy Parker, b. 1893*

August						
S	**M**	**T**	**W**	**T**	**F**	**S**
						1
2	3	4	5	6	7	8
9	10	11	12	13	14	15
16	17	18	19	20	21	22
23	24	25	26	27	28	29
30	31					

August
1998

September						
S	**M**	**T**	**W**	**T**	**F**	**S**
		1	2	3	4	5
6	7	8	9	10	11	12
13	14	15	16	17	18	19
20	21	22	23	24	25	26
27	28	29	30			

H. P. Lovecraft
August 20, 1890 - March 15, 1937

H. P. Lovecraft believed that "the oldest and strongest emotion of mankind is fear, and the oldest and strongest kind of fear is fear of the unknown." He sought to evoke that fear, and an atmosphere of horror and dread in his work. Using 14 pseudonyms as well as his own name, he composed spine-tingling short stories, novels, and poems. His stories have titles like "The Thing on the Doorstep," "The Rats in the Walls," and "The Whisperer in the Darkness."

He was a sickly, precocious child, who grew up in a Victorian mansion in Providence, Rhode Island. Too ill to attend school, he taught himself by reading history and Gothic horror stories. He called Edgar Allen Poe "my God of fiction."

In 1917, he began submitting his horror and fantasy tales to pulp magazines like *Weird Tales*. He also drew on his New England roots and wrote stories that focused on superstition and evil against a realistic background. His most popular tales belong to the "Cthulhu Mythos," a strange fictional universe of gods and legends and eerie landscapes. In 1936, he published *The Shadow Over Innsmouth*, the only book published during his lifetime.

After his death, his stories were collected and published by Arkham House, which was founded by Lovecraft's friend and fellow writer, August Derleth, who believed that Lovecraft was a "master of the macabre."

Other critics and writers disagreed. "A totally untalented and unreadable writer," wrote Larry McMurtry. Ursula Le Guin was even more scathing. "Lovecraft was an exceptionally, almost impeccably, bad writer," she said. "Derivative, inept, and callow, his tales can satisfy only those who believe that a capital letter, some words, and a full stop make a sentence."

Even Lovecraft knew that he was a bungling, amateurish writer. Still, between 1970 and 1973 over a million paperback copies of his books were sold. On Halloween, 1975, horror and fantasy writers and hundreds of Lovecraft's fans gathered in Providence, Rhode Island, to celebrate his work and tour the town where Lovecraft was born. During the 1960s and 1970s, filmakers translated several of his stories to the screen in *The Haunted Palace*, *Die, Monster, Die!*, and *The Dunwich Horror*.

Although Lovecraft was not a good writer, he was persistent in his strange vision. He wrote, he said, "not for praise." His goal was to "paint the scenes" that existed in his imagination. And, since he believed in a kind of "cosmic indifferentism," he painted his canvas with dark unknown horrors that elude rational interpretation.

Robertson Davies
August 28, 1913 - December 2, 1995

In photographs taken during his old age, Robertson Davies has a flowing silver beard and wears a wise and enigmatic expression, looking like a magus out of myth. A magician of the written word, during his long and productive life he wrote more than 30 volumes of fiction, and also plays, criticism, and essays. He worked in a study filled with objects that nurtured him—a part of an oak beam from his father's childhood home in Wales, a treasured photograph of Jung, an alabaster bust of the actor-manager Henry Irving, and the Davies coat-of-arms, a rampant winged dragon. The dragon reminded him of the "might and the chthonic force of the Unconscious."

Davies once said that the theme of all his work was "the isolation of the human spirit." As the youngest child (an "accident") unwanted by his older parents, he had a solitary childhood. His schoolmates tormented him, "bloody-minded riffraff" he called them. A bout with scarlet fever left him slightly deaf, but it also made him pay attention to what people said. He told himself stories, intoning the sentences aloud, and his parents taught him "there was only one word which would express a particular shade of meaning."

Coming to terms with his inner self and finding the right words to convey experience were his life-long struggles. Davies avenged himself on the bullies of his past and the dreary Ontario towns of his youth by transforming them into vivid characters and fictional landscapes, such as the popular *Deptford Trilogy* (*Fifth Business*, *The Manticore*, *World of Wonders*).

For 20 years, Davies served as master of Toronto's Massey College, and in his books he educated and entertained his readers, who learned about magic, circus troupes, gypsy culture, repairing violins, art forgery, theater production, and the insular life of small towns. The first Canadian writer who attracted an international audience (his books have been translated into 17 languages), he loved to satirize Canadian provincialism. Critic Michiko Kakutani observed that Davies' rich works functioned not only "as superbly funny entertainments but also give ... a deeper kind of pleasure—delight, awe, religious intimations, a fine sense of the past, and of the boundless depth and variety of life."

Davies said farewell to his readers in his last novel, *The Cunning Man*, published just months before he died. This is the "great Theater of Life," says his narrator. "Admission is free but the taxation is mortal. You come when you can, and leave when you must. The show is continuous. Good-night."

Sunday

23

Edgar Lee Masters, b. 1868

Monday

24

Jorge Luis Borges, b. 1899

Tuesday

25

Bret Harte, b. 1836

Wednesday

26

Thursday

27

Theodore Dreiser, b. 1871

Friday

28

Robertson Davies, b. 1913   Johann Wolfgang Goethe, b. 1749

Saturday

Maurice Maeterlinck, b. 1862   29

August						
S	M	T	W	T	F	S
						1
2	3	4	5	6	7	8
9	10	11	12	13	14	15
16	17	18	19	20	21	22
23	24	25	26	27	28	29
30	31					

August
1998

September						
S	M	T	W	T	F	S
		1	2	3	4	5
6	7	8	9	10	11	12
13	14	15	16	17	18	19
20	21	22	23	24	25	26
27	28	29	30			

Sunday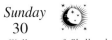
30
Mary Wollstonecraft Shelley, b. 1797

Monday
31

William Saroyan, b. 1908
Late Summer Holiday (U.K. ex. Scotland)

Tuesday
1

Edgar Rice Burroughs, b. 1875

Wednesday
2

Thursday
3

Sarah Orne Jewett, b. 1849

Friday
4

Mary Renault, b. 1905
Richard Wright, b. 1908
Antonin Artaud, b. 1896

Saturday
5

August						
S	M	T	W	T	F	S
						1
2	3	4	5	6	7	8
9	10	11	12	13	14	15
16	17	18	19	20	21	22
23	24	25	26	27	28	29
30	31					

August/September
1998

September						
S	M	T	W	T	F	S
		1	2	3	4	5
6	7	8	9	10	11	12
13	14	15	16	17	18	19
20	21	22	23	24	25	26
27	28	29	30			

Mary Renault
September 4, 1905 - December 12, 1983

Her novels about the history and mythology of Greece (*The King Must Die*, *The Persian Boy*, *The Mask of Apollo*) are so alive and immediate that the reader feels transported into that ancient world. How did she do it? "If you look at a collection of Greek vases," Mary Renault said, "you'll find all kinds of daily things ... All the little implements they have hanging up on the walls, or in the gymnasium or ... in the kitchen."

Two generals playing draughts: Greek vases revealed the details of daily life

Her research was impeccable. But her empathy and understanding of human nature, and her calm treatment of love—heterosexual, homosexual, or bisexual—as universal and distinctly individual, set her apart from other novelists of her time. Her novel *The Charioteer* (1955), which dealt with homosexuality and sexual identity, is considered her finest achievement.

The only child of a doctor, she was born Mary Challans and nicknamed Molly. Educated at St. Hugh's College, Oxford, she was taught by the great medievalist and writer J. R. R. Tolkien. At the Ashmolean Museum at Oxford, she saw a replica of the Cretan Bull-leaper, which she studied again and again. She wanted to write, but her early efforts were derivative, based on books instead of felt life.

In the summer of 1933, on a tour through the Cotswolds, she walked into Radcliffe Infirmary and announced that she wanted to become a nurse. Nursing, she decided, would give her real experience of life. Her first novel, *Purposes of Love*, which was set in a hospital and dealt with love between women, brought her a £50 advance, about the same as a year's salary for a nurse.

After writing a half-dozen or so well-received contemporary novels, she turned her attention to the ancient past. In 1947, she won a $150,000 MGM Award for her novel *Return to Night*. With her longtime companion Julie Mullard, she moved to Durban, South Africa, where she would live for the rest of her life.

To prepare her books, she traveled and studied extensively in Greece, northern Africa, and the Aegean Islands. Her novel *The King Must Die* (1958) began to take shape after her visit to the Palace of Knossos on Crete. "I began thinking about Theseus and wondered what it was like for a simple Bronze Age warrior to be confronted with this sophisticated metropolis," she said.

David Sweetman, her biographer, asked her once how she wanted to be remembered. "As someone who got it right," Renault replied.

Anna Cora Mowatt
September 12, 1819 - July 29, 1870

On a hot June evening in 1845, Anna Cora
Mowatt, then 26, sat in her dressing room at
the Park Theatre in New York City preparing
to make her professional acting debut. In the
dim glow of the gas lamp, the face she saw
in the mirror had the pale, bland features of a
well-bred society lady. After all, she was the
daughter of the wealthy merchant Samuel
Ogden and a member of one of New York's
oldest families. Anna spread out her make-up
supplies. First, she patted soft butter over her
face and then smoothed on a layer of
powdered vermilion for color. She lit a
candle and heated a steel knitting needle in
its flame. Working carefully and precisely,
she lined her large blue eyes with the soot
from the needle. With a burnt cork, she darkened her eyebrows. She blended a bit of
the vermilion with the butter and reddened her lips. To set the make-up, she dipped a
rabbit's foot in rice powder and dusted her face.

All of glittering New York society turned out for her debut, and it was a resounding
triumph. For the next eight years, she was the foremost actress of her time.

Anna Cora Mowatt brought respectability to the acting profession, but she is remembered today as America's first woman playwright. Her play *Fashion*, a comedy in five
acts, premiered at the Park Theatre just a few months before her acting debut. The
play, which satirizes New York society, enjoyed good reviews and played in cities
across America and in London. She had aimed for a "dramatic, not a literary, success,"
and it continues to be revived today.

The ninth child in a family of 14, Anna enjoyed a comfortable, privileged childhood.
As a girl she wrote doggerel and scattered her verses around the house and gardens for
her family to find. At 14, she translated a play by Voltaire. At 15, she eloped with 31-
year-old James Mowatt, a lawyer.

Perhaps because her husband encouraged her writing, the marriage was a happy one.
When he lost his fortune in 1841, Anna gave poetry readings to earn money, wrote
articles under a pen name, and published a best-selling book called *Housekeeping
Made Easy*.

Supporting herself and her husband was not easy. She was plagued by poor health
(which she treated with mesmeric seances), and she struggled financially throughout
her life. Yet she told a friend "there is an indescribable charm in active employment, in
feeling we are of use—which renders all hardship light."

Sunday
6

Monday
7

Elinor Wylie, b. 1885
Labor Day

Tuesday
8

Wednesday
9

Leo Tolstoy, b. 1828

Thursday
10

Hilda Doolittle, (H.D.), b. 1886

Friday
11

D.H. Lawrence, b. 1885
O. Henry, b. 1862

 Saturday
12

Anna Cora Mowatt, b. 1819

September						
S	M	T	W	T	F	S
		1	2	3	4	5
6	7	8	9	10	11	12
13	14	15	16	17	18	19
20	21	22	23	24	25	26
27	28	29	30			

September
1998

October						
S	M	T	W	T	F	S
				1	2	3
4	5	6	7	8	9	10
11	12	13	14	15	16	17
18	19	20	21	22	23	24
25	26	27	28	29	30	31

Sunday
13
Roald Dahl, b. 1916

Monday
14

Tuesday
15

Agatha Christie, b. 1890
James Fenimore Cooper, b. 1789

Wednesday
16

Emilia Pardo Bazán, b. 1851

Thursday
17

William Carlos Williams, b. 1883
U.S. Constitution adopted, 1787

Friday
18

Samuel Johnson, b. 1709

Saturday
19

September						
S	M	T	W	T	F	S
		1	2	3	4	5
6	7	8	9	10	11	12
13	14	15	16	17	18	19
20	21	22	23	24	25	26
27	28	29	30			

September
1998

October						
S	M	T	W	T	F	S
				1	2	3
4	5	6	7	8	9	10
11	12	13	14	15	16	17
18	19	20	21	22	23	24
25	26	27	28	29	30	31

Emilia Pardo Bazán
September 16, 1851 - May 12, 1921

"Men," she declared, "can hardly form an idea of how difficult it is for a woman to acquire culture and to fill in her education by teaching herself. Boys, from the age they can walk and talk, attend elementary schools, then the secondary institutes, the academies, the university. ... For them, all advantages. For women, all obstacles."

Emilia Pardo Bazán was luckier than most. Her father, a well-to-do member of the Galician gentry, encouraged her to read and study as a child. Later, she attended a French school in Madrid and made several pro-longed visits to Paris.

When she set out to become a writer, she devised a rigorous program of training. She studied English and Italian, read French novels and German philosophy, and developed what she described as "a liking for systematic, methodical and reflective reading, which goes beyond reading for pleasure and becomes study." Years afterward she remarked that "it is good, very good, to read everything during the period of study. Except that later on, one should remember only what is suitable—and what is very much of one's own land."

Pardo Bazán's novels, while influenced by French and Russian models, were very much a product of the Galician landscape where she spent most of her life. Her upstairs study in the city of La Coruña overlooked the coast of northern Spain on one side and the Church of Santiago on the other.

She wrote about the people of Galicia: aristocrats and peasants, schoolboys and middle-class wives and mothers. Convinced that the novel must above all be a serious undertaking, and inspired by the example of Zola, Pardo Bazán went to tobacco factories to research her 1883 novel, *The Woman Orator*. The book includes a graphic "obstetrical scene," whose presence prompted some critics to decry the work's poor taste.

Throughout her life Doña Emilia provoked controversy. In 1882 and 1883 she published a series of newspaper essays in defense of Naturalism, which led to a permanent breach in her marriage. She had a love affair with the most famous Spanish novelist of her time, Benito Pérez Galdós. In 1916, when she was appointed the first woman professor at Madrid's Central University, the all-male student population shunned her classes.

She grew accustomed to criticism. Against the woman writer, she said, "there is underlying and tenacious prejudice." To this day, Pardo Bazán's work—in particular *The House of Ulloa*, her virtuosic portrait of a decadent Galician aristocracy—proves her detractors wrong.

T. S. Eliot
September 26, 1888 - January 4, 1965

Those who met Tom Eliot for the first time were surprised by his size. He was a big man, just over six feet tall and slightly stooped, with (as he described himself in a mocking poem) "clerical cut" features—a grim brow and a prim mouth.

In literary terms, he was a giant. He distinguished himself as a poet, critic, playwright, and editor/publisher. While his greatness could rest on his poems alone—which include "The Love Song of J. Alfred Prufrock," "The Waste Land," *Ash Wednesday,* and *Four Quartets*—his critical essays helped form the bedrock of New Criticism, and his plays—*Sweeney Agonistes, Murder in the Cathedral, The Family Reunion*, and *The Cocktail Party*—have been equally influential.

In pop culture terms, he was a superstar. In 1948, he won the Nobel Prize for Literature; in 1950, he was on the cover of *Time* magazine; in 1956, 15,000 people attended one of his lectures; and today, millions have seen *Cats*, the spectacular musical, which Andrew Lloyd Webber adapted from Eliot's *Old Possum's Book of Practical Cats*.

Eliot loved cats. Presumably his cats curled up next to him while he wrote, lounging on his books, disturbing his papers, or purring with narcissistic contentment while he struggled to set down what he called the "general mess of imprecision of feeling."

With a superb education in philosophy and literature from Harvard University, Eliot wrote with elegant precision and incisive intelligence. "Poetry is not a turning loose of emotion," he said, "but an escape from emotion."

Some saw Eliot's intelligence as a curb on his art. Jorge Luis Borges believed that Robert Frost was a finer poet than Eliot because poetry is "beyond intelligence." Others find lines such as these, from Eliot's "Little Gidding" in *Four Quartets*, sublime: "We shall not cease from exploration / And the end of all our exploring / Will be to arrive where we started / And know the place for the first time."

His success and his intelligence could not immunize him against heartbreak or controversy. In 1915, he married Vivien Haigh-Wood, a young English girl, who, perhaps for undiagnosed physical reasons, descended into madness. Eliot separated from her in 1932, and she died in an institution in 1947.

Some of Eliot's writing expresses anti-Semitism, and his work has undergone a reassessment in the years following his death. At 70, Eliot assessed his own life. "I am just beginning to grow up, to get maturity," he said. "In the last few years everything I'd done up to 60 or so has seemed very childish."

Sunday
20

Stevie Smith, b. 1902   Upton Sinclair, b. 1879   Rosh Hashanah begins at sunset, Hebrew year 5759

Monday
21

H.G.Wells, b. 1866

Tuesday
22

Wednesday
23

Fall Equinox, 1:37 am EDT

Thursday
24

Frances Ellen Watkins Harper, b. 1825 [?]

Friday
25

Red Smith, b.1905
William Faulkner, b. 1897

Saturday

T. S. Eliot, b. 1888   **26**

September						
S	M	T	W	T	F	S
	1	2	3	4	5	
6	7	8	9	10	11	12
13	14	15	16	17	18	19
20	21	22	23	24	25	26
27	28	29	30			

September
1998

October						
S	M	T	W	T	F	S
				1	2	3
4	5	6	7	8	9	10
11	12	13	14	15	16	17
18	19	20	21	22	23	24
25	26	27	28	29	30	31

Sunday
27
Grazia Deledda, b. 1871

Monday
28

Elmer Rice, b. 1892

Tuesday
29

Miguel de Unamuno, b. 1864
Miguel de Cervantes Saavedra, b. 1547
Elizabeth Gaskell, b. 1810
Yom Kippur begins at sunset

Wednesday
30

Truman Capote, b. 1924

Thursday
1

Friday
2

Wallace Stevens, b. 1879

Saturday
3   *Thomas Wolfe, b. 1900*

September						
S	M	T	W	T	F	S
		1	2	3	4	5
6	7	8	9	10	11	12
13	14	15	16	17	18	19
20	21	22	23	24	25	26
27	28	29	30			

September/October
1998

October						
S	M	T	W	T	F	S
				1	2	3
4	5	6	7	8	9	10
11	12	13	14	15	16	17
18	19	20	21	22	23	24
25	26	27	28	29	30	31

Elmer Rice
September 28, 1892 - May 8, 1967

In a walk-up on 90th Street in New York
City, Elmer Leopold Reizenstein daydreamed
over German picture books and learned to
read English from the newspaper funnies.
"Literature was as alien to my family's world
as were the other arts," he recalled. "There
was never a book in my home until I
introduced one."

Forced by poverty to quit school at 14, Rice
worked as a law clerk, while earning his
high-school diploma and attending New York
Law School. After reading George Bernard
Shaw's *Plays, Pleasant and Unpleasant*,
Rice became convinced of the "evils of the
capitalist system," and embarked on a
playwriting career.

*Elmer Rice and his daughter, Margaret, arriving
in New York aboard the S.S. Champlain in 1933.*

"A writer, if he is not plagued by economic worries," Rice asserted, "is about as
independent as anyone can be." Committed to an idealistic rather than practical
socialism, Rice often wrote from "no nobler impulse than a realistic desire to make a
comfortable living." His first play, *On Trial* (1914), which he called a "shrewd piece
of stage carpentry," ran for a year on Broadway and earned him $100,000. In his half-
century career, Rice wrote 50 full-length plays, four novels, short stories, one-act
plays, scripts for television, radio, and film, and an autobiography. *Street Scene*
(1929), a panorama play about New York life, won the Pulitzer Prize.

Rice's reputation rests, though, on his finest play, *The Adding Machine* (1923).
Following trips to the Ford Motor Company in Detroit and to the Chicago stockyards,
where he observed monotonous industrialism, Rice saw a vision of the play he
wanted to write as if "a switch had been turned on." He wrote it in 17 days. Using the
techniques of German expressionism, Rice depicted the universe as a cosmic business.
The leading character, a bookkeeper named Mr. Zero, kills his boss after he learns that
he has been replaced by an adding machine.

A short, pugnacious man with red hair, Rice served for many years on the board of the
American Civil Liberties Union. He was president of the Authors League and founder
of the Dramatists Guild. Disenchanted with Broadway producers, he and four other
writers formed the Playwrights' Company to produce their own work.

During World War II, Rice divorced his first wife and married Betty Field, a young
actress, who inspired his lovely 1945 comedy, *Dream Girl*. Rice confessed that for the
first time his personal happiness had overshadowed political issues.

At the end of his life, he lamented the scarcity of good playwrights, but he believed
that "so long as people continue to dream and to dramatize themselves there will
be theater."

Ken Saro-Wiwa
October 10, 1941 - November 10, 1995

He stood no more than five foot two or three. Small and energetic, he had a broad grin and a mordant tongue. He smoked a pipe with a curved stem. Nigerians recognized Ken Saro-Wiwa by his pipe.

He was born in southeastern Nigeria, in the Ogoni homeland. Between the ages of 13 and 20 he attended school at the prestigious Government College Umuahia, where he took part in competitions to see who could read the most books. He also helped write, edit, and publish school magazines.

He was forced to abandon his drama studies in college because of political strife, which by 1967 had turned into civil war. Twenty years later he wrote about his war experiences in the memoir *On a Darkling Plain*.

War, and the follies and corruption of Nigerian politics and society, informed much of what Ken Saro-Wiwa thought, said, and wrote. In perhaps his finest book, *Sozaboy* (1985), Saro-Wiwa forged an idiosyncratic blend of Nigerian pidgin, broken English, and what author and friend William Boyd terms an "altogether more classical and lyrical English" to tell the story of a village boy recruited into the Biafran Army during the civil war. The book is subtitled "A Novel in Rotten English." Boyd calls it "a great antiwar novel—among the very best of the twentieth century."

In the late 1980s, Saro-Wiwa became increasingly involved in the fight to rescue his homeland from ecological devastation. Since the mid-1950s, international oil companies, in complicity with the Nigerian government, had plundered Ogoniland, and what was once a peaceful farming and fishing community had become a poisoned wasteland.

His activism led to Saro-Wiwa's arrest in 1993. Charged with treason, he was held prisoner for several months, then released. The following year he was again arrested, and along with several others was accused of plotting to murder four men during a rally in an Ogoni town. Saro-Wiwa was innocent.

He spent more than a year in jail. In 1995 he and his co-defendants were tried before a specially convened tribunal. It was a show trial, with a pre-ordained verdict. The defendants were sentenced to death. On November 10, 1995, Ken Saro-Wiwa and eight others were hanged.

Newsreel pictures from the final days of his trial show Saro-Wiwa leaning on a stick as he walks toward the courthouse, gaunt and aged as a result of his long incarceration. Between his teeth he grips a pipe with a curved stem.

Sunday

4

Edward Stratemeyer, b. 1862   *Damon Runyon, b. 1884*

 Monday

5

Tuesday

6

Caroline Gordon, b. 1895

Wednesday

7

Thursday

8

Friday

9

Bruce Catton, b. 1899

Saturday

Ken Saro-Wiwa, b. 1941   10

October						
S	M	T	W	T	F	S
				1	2	3
4	5	6	7	8	9	10
11	12	13	14	15	16	17
18	19	20	21	22	23	24
25	26	27	28	29	30	31

October
1998

November						
S	M	T	W	T	F	S
1	2	3	4	5	6	7
8	9	10	11	12	13	14
15	16	17	18	19	20	21
22	23	24	25	26	27	28
29	30					

Sunday
11

Eleanor Roosevelt, b. 1884

Monday
12

Columbus Day
Thanksgiving Day (Canada)

Tuesday
13

Wednesday
14

Hannah Arendt, b. 1906
Katherine Mansfield, b. 1888
e. e. cummings, b. 1894

Thursday
15

Virgil, b. 70 B.C.

Friday
16

Oscar Wilde, b. 1854
Eugene O'Neill, b. 1888
Noah Webster, b. 1758

Saturday
17   *Elinor Glyn, b. 1864*

| October |
S	M	T	W	T	F	S
				1	2	3
4	5	6	7	8	9	10
11	12	13	14	15	16	17
18	19	20	21	22	23	24
25	26	27	28	29	30	31

October
1998

| November |
S	M	T	W	T	F	S
1	2	3	4	5	6	7
8	9	10	11	12	13	14
15	16	17	18	19	20	21
22	23	24	25	26	27	28
29	30					

Elinor Glyn
October 17, 1864 - September 23, 1943

In 1907, with the publication of her sixth
novel, *Three Weeks*, Elinor Glyn became one
of the most talked-about writers in the world.
Throughout New York and London society,
people repeated a rhyme based on the
novel's central scene, in which the heroine,
lounging seductively on a tiger skin,
seduces the hero:

> Would you like to sin
> with Elinor Glyn
> on a tiger skin?
> Or would you prefer
> to err with her
> on some other fur?

She was beautiful, vain, and calculating. She married Clayton Glyn, a wealthy British
sportsman, for his social connections. She wrote books for money—and because she
wanted to impart her experience of "romance" to millions of ordinary men and
women. "Romance," she explained, "is a spiritual disguise created by the imagination
to envelop material happenings and desires, so that they may be in greater harmony
with the soul."

In order to create her novels, she drew shamelessly from her own life and from the
lives and intrigues of her aristocratic friends and acquaintances. A visit to Russia in
1909 led to Glyn's 1910 novel, *His Hour*, in which a young English widow is courted
in St. Petersburg by a Russian prince. The book included a thinly disguised account of
Elinor's own romantic encounter with a handsome guardsman, and her near-kidnap-
ping while passing through Warsaw en route to Moscow.

To those who accused her of bad writing and immoral plots, Glyn countered that her
books were "the outpouring of my whole nature, romantic, proud, and passionate, but
forever repressed in real life by the barriers of custom and tradition."

In 1920 she went to Hollywood to write screenplays. "If Hollywood hadn't existed,
Elinor Glyn would have had to invent it," said fellow screenwriter Anita Loos. Glyn
adapted several of her own novels to the screen and also wrote a number of original
scripts. To actors and directors, she strutted her superior knowledge of costumes,
make-up, sets, and theatrical movement. Claiming that American males did not know
how to kiss, she proceeded to demonstrate the proper technique.

Her celebrity declined sharply after 1927. Glyn spent her last decades living in
England, in semiseclusion. She blamed the demise of traditional society, "in the old
meaning of the word," on "the power of money." Paradoxically, it was money's power
that in large part created the phenomenon of Elinor Glyn.

Fannie Hurst
October 19, 1889 - February 23, 1968

"How did a writer know she was one?"
Fannie Hurst often asked herself. Did
isolation make a writer, she wondered. When
she was four, her sister Edna died of
diphtheria, leaving Fannie an only child.
Words became her refuge. She called herself
a "word lapidary ... ruby was a word that
glowed. Serene was like a pearl." Through
books, she escaped from her old-fashioned
parents, who did not understand her, and
from all the other little girls in St. Louis who
seemed to be thin, because she "was fat ...
and we were Jews. Almost everybody was
not Jewish."

Her father encouraged her to continue her
education at Washington University, and her vital, eccentric mother ("I yearned for the
power to write her in full dimension, but my pen clogs") provided a challenge to
Hurst's creative powers and stimulated her lifelong interest in capturing the texture of
women's lives.

At 14, Hurst began submitting her stories to the *Saturday Evening Post*, and secured
so many rejections that the *Post* began returning them "in batches." After college, she
moved to New York and supported herself at various odd jobs. She deluged magazine
editorial offices with her stories. Finally, the *Post* accepted her 36th story, and her first
book of short stories, *Just Around the Corner*, was published in 1914.

She wrote primarily about women, women in bad marriages, women in dead-end jobs,
lonely women confined by circumstances, and it annoyed her that she became
pigeonholed as a woman's writer. Still, she enjoyed liking women, she said, because
she "admired the curve in all of nature's processes." Hurst had a gift for detail and
description. In one short story, she observed that the women in the "hothouse garden"
at the Hotel Bon Ton never had a broken fingernail "or that little brash place along the
forefinger that tattles so of potato peeling or asparagus scraping."

During the 1920s and 1930s, Hurst was prolific and highly paid, earning the top price
of $5,000 for a single story. Her productivity (she authored 18 novels and hundreds of
short stories) and her mass appeal were offered as proofs of her lack of stature. She
was never a favorite of the critics, who, while they applauded her gift for characteriza-
tion, objected to her sentimentality. Hurst claimed that she would have preferred
"classic failure to a popular success."

She realized, though, that she had little choice in the matter. "There is no adequate
definition for creative writing," she wrote, "any more than it is possible to describe
pain or flavor or color."

Sunday
18

Monday
19

Fannie Hurst, b. 1889

 Tuesday
20

Arthur Rimbaud, b. 1854

Wednesday
21

Samuel Taylor Coleridge, b. 1772

Thursday
22

Friday
23

Saturday
Moss Hart, b. 1904   24

October						
S	**M**	**T**	**W**	**T**	**F**	**S**
				1	2	3
4	5	6	7	8	9	10
11	12	13	14	15	16	17
18	19	20	21	22	23	24
25	26	27	28	29	30	31

October
1998

November						
S	**M**	**T**	**W**	**T**	**F**	**S**
1	2	3	4	5	6	7
8	9	10	11	12	13	14
15	16	17	18	19	20	21
22	23	24	25	26	27	28
29	30					

Sunday

25

Daylight Saving Time ends

Monday

26

Tuesday

27

Sylvia Plath, b. 1932
Dylan Thomas, b. 1914

Wednesday

28

Evelyn Waugh, b. 1903

Thursday

29

James Boswell, b. 1740
Jean Giraudoux, b. 1882

Friday

30

Ezra Pound, b. 1885

Saturday

31   Halloween   *John Keats, b. 1795*   *Mary Wilkins Freeman, b. 1852*

		October				
S	M	T	W	T	F	S
				1	2	3
4	5	6	7	8	9	10
11	12	13	14	15	16	17
18	19	20	21	22	23	24
25	26	27	28	29	30	31

October
1998

		November				
S	M	T	W	T	F	S
1	2	3	4	5	6	7
8	9	10	11	12	13	14
15	16	17	18	19	20	21
22	23	24	25	26	27	28
29	30					

Mary Wilkins Freeman
October 31, 1852 - 1930

A frail, blonde child, derided as "little, dolly-inky-rosy," by her classmates, Mary Wilkins possessed an iron will. "It is never from anything but a sense of duty that I commence to write," she told a friend. She also wrote from necessity.

From the backyard of her family home in Brattleboro, Vermont, Mary could look up the wooded hill and see the Vermont Insane Asylum and the institution's cemetery. It was her first glimpse of "psychic terror." Her father worried that she had no talent and wondered how she would make a living.

She tried teaching, but soon found that she cared "little for her pupils." She liked painting, but brushes and paints were too expensive.

Since she loved to read, Mary turned next to writing. She was elated when a children's magazine paid her $20 for two religious poems. When *Harper's Bazaar* accepted her short story "Two Old Lovers," she was on her way to becoming one of the most prolific, most successful writers of her time, producing almost 250 short stories, 14 novels, several plays, poems, and non-fiction pieces.

Like her most famous character, Louisa Ellis in "A New England Nun," Freeman was devoted to routine and order. For years she lived with her childhood friend Mary John Wales, who managed the practical details of her life and thus gave Wilkins time to write. Mary John "shuts me in my study each morning, and won't let me out until I have written at least fifteen hundred words," she said.

In her stories, Wilkins paid careful attention to clothing, sewing, cooking, and housework, all the mundane details of a woman's life. She probed beneath the surface of her characters' lives to discover "records of sin and agony, courage and pride, loss of faith. Nothing is glossed over." She became indignant, though, when her publishers expected her to resemble the women in her stories, to be "attired in my best black silk and living ... in a little white New England cottage."

While her New England nun character followed a path so straight and narrow "that there was no room for anyone at her side," when she was 49, Wilkins married Dr. Charles Freeman. In 1907 they built a beautiful home in Metuchen, New Jersey, called "Freewarren," but by 1921 Dr. Freeman had become a dangerous alcoholic and drug addict. He was judged mentally incompetent and Mary had him committed to the New Jersey State Hospital for the Insane.

"I must have a very tough streak in me," Mary wrote. "I did not look so but time has proved it."

The Political Memoir

When Harry Truman left the White House in 1953, he signed a $600,000 contract with Time-Life, Inc., to produce a publishable, 300,000-word manuscript of his memoirs. He promptly hired a small team of writers and researchers, and with the help of a gold-plated recording machine supplied by Time, Inc., he set out to record his memories of the presidency. But the first draft of the project so disappointed him that Truman likened it to a *Saturday Evening Post* story: "My Life and Happy Times in the White House." He told a friend he wanted to write history, not fiction.

Frederick The Great

Centuries earlier, the same impulse spurred a Greek general named Thucydides, and a pair of Roman statesmen named Julius and Augustus Caesar, to recall wars and events in which they had played a role. "There is properly no history," said Emerson, "only biography."

The oldest historical records in China chronicle court events. In time, such record-keeping evolved into formal genres. The "Diary of Activity and Repose," for instance, tracked the emperor's activities by day and by night. In feudal Japan, palace officials kept diaries so as to maintain a "minute recording of correct ceremonial" procedure.

In the West, the political memoir emerged as an art form in the 15th century, with the appearance of Philippe de Commynes' stylish *Memoirs*, a record of the courtier's service to Charles the Bold and Louis XI of France. Blending political, historical, and autobiographical anecdote, Commynes produced an insightful and sensitive portrait of his age.

In the 1890s, at least 43 houses competed for the privilege of publishing Otto von Bismarck's memoirs. The ex-Chancellor collaborated on the project with his long-time secretary, Lothar Bucher. An acquaintance described the pair at work: Bucher sat peevishly at a table with a blank sheet of paper, "sharp of ear," while Bismarck reclined on a chaise longue, reading the newspaper. "The prince said not a word, Bucher even less—and the page remained blank."

Frederick the Great of Prussia had an easier time of it. The process of writing his memoirs, he said, "occupies me, diverts me, and makes me fitter for work."

Throughout history, leaders have seemed to understand instinctively that by recording their lives, they can shape their legacy. Richard Nixon resurrected himself—repeatedly—through words. "To control the present is to control the past," wrote George Orwell. "To control the past is to control the future."

Sunday

1

Stephen Crane, b. 1871

Monday

2

Tuesday

3

 Wednesday

4

Ivan Sergeyevich Turgenev, b. 1816
Will Rogers, b. 1879

Thursday

5

Friday

6

Saturday

7

Albert Camus, b. 1913

November						
S	M	T	W	T	F	S
1	2	3	4	5	6	7
8	9	10	11	12	13	14
15	16	17	18	19	20	21
22	23	24	25	26	27	28
29	30					

November
1998

December						
S	M	T	W	T	F	S
		1	2	3	4	5
6	7	8	9	10	11	12
13	14	15	16	17	18	19
20	21	22	23	24	25	26
27	28	29	30	31		

Sunday
8
Margaret Mitchell, b. 1900

Monday
9

Anne Sexton, b. 1928

Tuesday
10

Wednesday
11

Feodor Dostoevsky, b. 1821
Veterans' Day
Remembrance Day (Canada)

Thursday
12

Sor Juana Inés de la Cruz, b. 1651
Elizabeth Cady Stanton, b. 1815

Friday
13

Saint Augustine, b. 354

Saturday
14   *Constance Rourke, b. 1885*

November						
S	M	T	W	T	F	S
1	2	3	4	5	6	7
8	9	10	11	12	13	14
15	16	17	18	19	20	21
22	23	24	25	26	27	28
29	30					

November
1998

December						
S	M	T	W	T	F	S
		1	2	3	4	5
6	7	8	9	10	11	12
13	14	15	16	17	18	19
20	21	22	23	24	25	26
27	28	29	30	31		

Constance Rourke
November 14, 1885 - March 23, 1941

At a young age, Constance Rourke announced that she intended "to marry, have a baby, and get a divorce at 35." In fact, Rourke never married. Instead, she devoted herself to her mother—a dour, rigid, and by most accounts tyrannical figure.

The two women were effectively forced on one another after Rourke's father died, from tuberculosis, in 1888. Constance was barely three years old. In the wake of her father's death, she and her mother moved to Grand Rapids, Michigan, where they remained for the rest of their lives.

In high school, Rourke was a bookish, aloof, unfashionable young woman with no "real friends." She joined the Library Society and the basketball club. She went on to study at Vassar, where she pursued a degree in English literature and, like her schoolteacher mother, developed an abiding interest in education and its power to shape society. She began to view writing as "revolutionary," because it not only sprang from social conditions, but could alter them.

For a period of several years she tried her hand at teaching, but ultimately concluded that she must do "a certain amount of creative work. This as far as I can see is incompatible with a 'career' as a teacher." She began writing essays and lectures on education. She also attempted poetry and fiction. Freelance writing, she discovered, allowed her to arrange her time in an "elastic" fashion.

Her great interest was American culture. In 1919 *The New Republic* published her first full-length article, an essay on vaudeville. Further essays, reviews, and stories followed. In 1931, she achieved national status as a critic of American arts with her book-length study of native wit, *American Humor.*

Her mother read and criticized all of Rourke's work before it was published. Throughout her life, Rourke credited her mother with her success and referred to her books and articles as joint ventures. "We mustn't mind being called 'cynical,'" she told her mother once after receiving a negative review.

By 1938, Rourke was immersed in research for a multivolume *History of American Culture.* On thousands of small blue slips of paper, she recorded notes on paintings, scrimshaw, cigar-store Indians, Shaker furniture, and other quintessentially American artifacts.

She never completed the project. One winter night in 1941, she slipped on a patch of ice and broke a vertebra. Days later she collapsed and died of an embolism. Constance Rourke is buried beside her mother in a family plot in Grand Rapids.

Thomas Chatterton

November 20, 1752 -
August 24, 1770

When he was seven, Thomas
Chatterton's mother gave him
some scraps of manuscript that
had been found in the ancient
church of St. Mary Redcliffe,
in the boy's native Bristol.
Chatterton told his mother that
she had discovered "a treasure,"
that he was "so glad, nothing
could be like it." "He fell in
love," Sarah Chatterton recalled.

Beguiled by antiquity, Chatterton began writing poems. At age eight, he was appren-
ticed to a local lawyer as a copy clerk. When his master found the child writing verse
on the job, he beat him and tore up his poems. Thomas Chatterton went on writing.

At the age of 15 or 16, he composed a sequence of poems purportedly written by a
15th-century monk named Rowley. Chatterton copied the works onto parchment
sheets and distributed them to Bristol acquaintances—among them William Barrett, a
local historian who cited Chatterton's Rowley material as a genuine source in his 1789
History of Bristol.

Chatterton duped a local pewterer into buying a fraudulent manuscript, and he nearly
persuaded Horace Walpole to publish a Rowley work on painting entitled "The Rise of
Peyncteynge yn Englande, wroten bie T. Rowleie, 1469." "Give me leave to ask you
where Rowley's poems are to be found. I should not be sorry to print them, or at least
a specimen of them, if they have never been printed," wrote Walpole, before discover-
ing Chatterton's hoax and brusquely dismissing him. Chatterton responded with a
poem in which he ridiculed Walpole's "Prosy Chapters" and "twaddling Letters," and
vowed to "live and stand / By Rowley's side—when Thou are dead and damned."

In April 1770, Chatterton shed the drudgery of his Bristol apprenticeship and fled to
London, with its promise of literary life. He never returned home. Between April and
August of that year, he wrote poetry, political essays, letters, and an autobiographical
Memoirs of a Sad Dog, in which he traces a young man's declining fortunes.

Although several magazines published his work, Chatterton could not earn enough to
sustain him. On August 24, 1770, his landlady raised his rent. Later that night, he
swallowed a solution of arsenic and water and died. Thomas Chatterton was
17 years old.

Within a decade of his death, works by and about Thomas Chatterton began to appear.
His meteoric life and dramatic death inspired a generation of Romantics. To this day
Chatterton remains, as William Wordsworth described him, "the marvellous Boy, /
The sleepless Soul that perished in his pride."

Sunday

15

Marianne Moore, b. 1887

Monday

16

George S. Kaufman, b. 1889

Tuesday

17

 Wednesday

18

W. S. Gilbert, b. 1836

Thursday

19

Friday

20

Thomas Chatterton, b. 1752   *Selma Lagerlöf, b. 1858*

Saturday

Voltaire, b. 1694   21

November						
S	M	T	W	T	F	S
1	2	3	4	5	6	7
8	9	10	11	12	13	14
15	16	17	18	19	20	21
22	23	24	25	26	27	28
29	30					

November
1998

December						
S	M	T	W	T	F	S
		1	2	3	4	5
6	7	8	9	10	11	12
13	14	15	16	17	18	19
20	21	22	23	24	25	26
27	28	29	30	31		

Sunday
22
George Eliot, b. 1819

Monday
23

Tuesday
24

Wednesday
25

Lope de Vega, b. 1562

Thursday
26

Eugene Ionesco, b. 1912
Thanksgiving Day

Friday
27

Fanny Kemble, b. 1809

Saturday
28   Brooks Atkinson, b. 1894

November						
S	M	T	W	T	F	S
1	2	3	4	5	6	7
8	9	10	11	12	13	14
15	16	17	18	19	20	21
22	23	24	25	26	27	28
29	30					

November
1998

December						
S	M	T	W	T	F	S
		1	2	3	4	5
6	7	8	9	10	11	12
13	14	15	16	17	18	19
20	21	22	23	24	25	26
27	28	29	30	31		

Brooks Atkinson
November 28, 1894 - January 13, 1984

Brooks Atkinson descended from a long line
of English Puritans. He grew up in Melrose,
Massachusetts, a place, he said, where
"worldly pleasures did not come easily
within the scope of our lives." It's remarkable and inexplicable that he would become
one of the most powerful and most beloved
theater critics of the 20th century.

Atkinson's father, a self-educated man, filled
his bookshelves with Shakespeare, Dickens,
Balzac, George Sand, and Walt Whitman.
When he entered Harvard College, Atkinson
discovered that he had already read all the
assigned freshman reading.

Books gave him entry into a world "of great size, mystery, and splendor," but he gave
his heart to newspapers. At eight, he edited and printed his own magazine called *The
Watchout*. He set up a print shop in his parents' rough attic. Printing seemed to him
"the most admirable of the crafts. It could be an art; it could be beautiful. It was also a
form of communication."

He learned the art of theater criticism from the legendary H. T. Parker at the *Boston
Transcript*. In 1925, Atkinson became drama critic of the *New York Times*, a post he
filled until 1960. He ushered in the modern era in American drama, championing the
plays of Eugene O'Neill, Lillian Hellman, Tennessee Williams, Sean O'Casey, Arthur
Miller, and Edward Albee. He traveled to Dallas, Texas, and supported the resident
theater movement begun by Margo Jones. While other critics ignored off-Broadway,
Atkinson went to downtown attics, lofts, and basements to see theater and then write
about it.

During World War II, he worked as a foreign correspondent in China and Russia and
earned a Pulitzer Prize. In addition to his reviews, he wrote a number of excellent
books about the theater, including *Broadway* (1970) and several books of essays. His
style is deceptively simple, relying on the power of the declarative sentence, the apt
simile, and the perfect adjective.

He composed his reviews in his head on the way out of the theater. When he got to his
office cubicle, he would light his pipe, prop up the playbill, and write out the review in
pencil on a ruled yellow pad.

Atkinson lauded "authors, directors, and actors who do the only work that keeps the
theater going" and he dismissed his own influence. He called his work the "pleasantest
job in the world."

When he retired, a friend remarked that the *Times* without Brooks Atkinson was "like
a bird without a warble."

Anna Comnena
December 2, 1083 - [1153?]

She looked like her father, Alexios, the emperor of Byzantium from 1081 to 1118. A friend was to remember Anna Comnena's large eyes, rainbow-like eyebrows, white skin, and face—"a perfectly chiseled circle. ... Her body was like a lyre or like a well-harmonized guitar, a fine instrument for a fine soul."

In her 15-volume history of her father's reign, Anna Comnena described her own birth, "in the room which had of old been set apart for the Empresses' confinements. Our forefathers called it the 'purple' room." Purple signified royalty, a fact that Anna never forgot. As first-born, she stood to inherit her father's throne.

It was Comnena's fate never to see her likeness on a Byzantine coin like this one

When she was just a few days old, her parents gave her a crown and a royal diadem. They betrothed her to her seven-year-old cousin, Constantine, who ruled as co-emperor with Anna's father. She was placed immediately under the care and tutelage of her fiancé's mother.

Her education was uncommon. She carried her study of Greek "to the highest pitch," as she phrased it. She learned rhetoric, perused the works of Aristotle and Plato, read the classics, studied science and philosophy. At 13, unbeknownst to her parents, she took grammar lessons from a palace eunuch. Her aptitude for medicine was so keen that in adulthood she was often asked to diagnose the condition of family members and to "adjudge the physicians' arguments."

Anna Comnena was 35 when her father died. Her younger brother John ascended to the throne. Convinced that he lacked the skill to govern, Anna conspired with others—including their mother—to assassinate the new emperor. The plot failed, and Anna spent most of her remaining years living in a convent far removed from the intrigues of palace life.

At 65, she began writing her father's history. She modelled her *Alexiad* on classical sources: Homer, Thucydides, Herodotus. Replete with biblical references, medical advice, court documents, and evocative portraits of Alexios and his colleagues and family, Anna Comnena's massive history comprises what one historian has called "the very tableau of the Byzantine empire under Alexios I."

In order to write the *Alexiad*, Anna drew on personal memory, interviews with soldiers who had accompanied her father on military campaigns, family accounts, state archives, diplomatic correspondence, and imperial decrees. The *Alexiad* is a model of early historiography. And yet, despite her achievement, Anna Comnena mourned one thing in life—"that she was never able, with all her dexterity, to acquire the Kingship."

Sunday

29

C. S. Lewis, b. 1898   Louisa May Alcott, b. 1832

Monday

30

Jonathan Swift, b. 1667   Mark Twain, b. 1835   Lucy Maud Montgomery, b. 1874

Tuesday

1

Wednesday

2

Anna Comnena, b. 1083

 Thursday

3

Friday

4

Rainer Maria Rilke, b. 1875

Saturday

5

	November					
S	M	T	W	T	F	S
1	2	3	4	5	6	7
8	9	10	11	12	13	14
15	16	17	18	19	20	21
22	23	24	25	26	27	28
29	30					

November/December
1998

	December					
S	M	T	W	T	F	S
		1	2	3	4	5
6	7	8	9	10	11	12
13	14	15	16	17	18	19
20	21	22	23	24	25	26
27	28	29	30	31		

Sunday

6

Susannah Moodie, b. 1803   Ira Gershwin, b. 1896

Monday

7

Willa Cather, b. 1873
Pearl Harbor Day

Tuesday

8

James Thurber, b. 1894

Wednesday

9

Thursday

10

Emily Dickinson, b. 1830

Friday

11

Saturday

12   Gustave Flaubert, b. 1821

December

S	M	T	W	T	F	S
		1	2	3	4	5
6	7	8	9	10	11	12
13	14	15	16	17	18	19
20	21	22	23	24	25	26
27	28	29	30	31		

December
1998

January 1999

S	M	T	W	T	F	S
					1	2
3	4	5	6	7	8	9
10	11	12	13	14	15	16
17	18	19	20	21	22	23
24	25	26	27	28	29	30
31						

Ira Gershwin
December 6, 1896 - August 17, 1983

When asked which came first, the words or the music, Ira Gershwin quipped, "The contract."

Actually, Ira couldn't read music. "I hit on a new tune," George Gershwin explained, "and play it for Ira and he hums it all over the place for a while till he gets an idea for a lyric. Then we work the thing out together."

Israel Gershwin was born on New York's Lower East Side to Jewish immigrant parents. His father was an enterprising but incompetent businessman who moved his family some 28 times while Ira was growing up. When Ira was ten, he began taking piano lessons, but since he preferred reading, he let his younger brother George monopolize the piano. As a teenager, Ira wrote French verse, experimenting with the triolet, the villanelle, and the rondeau. He kept scrapbooks of his favorite poems and collected poetry anthologies.

The first song the Gershwin brothers wrote together was "Waiting for the Sun to Come Out," in 1920, and their first Broadway hit was *Lady Be Good!* (1924). Other hits followed—*Tip Toes, Oh Kay, Funny Face.* On opening night of *Girl Crazy* (1930), which introduced "I Got Rhythm," George gave Ira a silver cigarette lighter with the inscription, "To Ira, the Words, from George, the Music." In 1932, Ira's words for *Of Thee I Sing* won the Pulitzer Prize for drama, making him the first lyricist to win that honor.

Dubose Heyward, who wrote the novel *Porgy*, which the Gershwins adapted into the great folk opera *Porgy and Bess*, recalled that "the brothers Gershwin ... would get at the piano, pound, wrangle, swear, burst into weird snatches of song, and eventually emerge with a polished lyric." Because of his gemlike lyrics, Ira was nicknamed "the Jeweller." A good lyric, he said, should be "rhymed conversation."

His brother inspired him. "He was always full of new ideas," Ira said, "and he was so good a musician, that I could do things with lyrics that I couldn't do with just a songwriter."

When George died suddenly at 38, Ira was shattered and unable to work. In 1940, Moss Hart convinced him to collaborate on the musical *Lady in the Dark.* In 1954, with Harold Arlen, Ira wrote *A Star is Born*, creating the memorable song "The Man That Got Away" for Judy Garland.

In his last years, Ira surrounded himself with Gershwin memorabilia, including his brother's favorite Steinway grand, and devoted himself to editing, compiling, and annotating his brother's works.

Heinrich Heine
December 13, 1797 or 1798 -
February 17, 1856

At first his uncle set him up in business, but within a year Heinrich Heine went broke. Subsidized again by his rich Uncle Salomon, he tried his hand at law. But he failed at it, too. Finally, Heine turned to history and literature. He became a writer—the most popular in his country since Goethe.

But until he was 40, Heine continued to receive his uncle's grudging financial assistance. After Salomon's death, Heine's cousin Carl struck a bargain with the writer: if Heine agreed to publish nothing about any member of the Heine family, Carl would pay him a pension for life. Heine agreed.

His first published poems and plays established him as a young Romantic. His liberal politics, as expressed in poems and articles, incurred the wrath of the Prussian government. In 1831, authorities banned two of Heine's books. Fearing arrest, and drawn to the ideals of the French Revolution, Heine went into exile in Paris, where he felt "like a fish in the water," he said.

In 1834 he met 19-year-old Crescence Eugénie Mirat, a near-illiterate shopgirl whom Heine christened "Mathilde" and married in 1841. He called her a "sweet, fat child." She knew nothing of Heine's fame and never read his work. She spent her time shopping and tending to her beloved parrot.

Mathilde remained with Heine throughout the debilitating, eight-year illness which ultimately claimed his life. To this day, the precise nature of Heine's ailment is unknown. What is known is that its symptoms reduced the poet to a 70-pound skeleton racked by excruciating pain, his eyelids and lower extremities paralyzed, his body confined for years to a "mattress tomb."

Heine bore his torture with "a serenity" that even he found incomprehensible. Unable to sleep at night, he composed poems and articles whose grandeur transcends anything he had written before. When he repeated his verse to himself, Heine found that it had a curious ability to relieve his pain. With a secretary's help, he spent hours polishing his poems. "Every present and past tense was probed and weighed, every obsolete or unusual word questioned, every superfluous adjective cut out," the secretary recalled. During his last months, Heine continued writing, scribbling poems in foot-high letters.

He remarked once that he did not wish to be buried in the suburbs of Paris, because "the cemetery there has got to be real boring." He preferred Montmartre. Heine's epitaph reads simply, "German poet."

Sunday
13
Heinrich Heine, b. 1797　　Chanukkah begins at sunset

Monday
14

Shirley Jackson, b. 1919

Tuesday
15

Maxwell Anderson, b. 1888

Wednesday
16

Jane Austen, b. 1775
Noel Coward, b. 1899

Thursday
17

Ford Madox Ford, b. 1873

 Friday
18

H.H. Munro (Saki), b. 1870

Saturday
Jean Genet, b. 1910　　## 19

December						
S	M	T	W	T	F	S
		1	2	3	4	5
6	7	8	9	10	11	12
13	14	15	16	17	18	19
20	21	22	23	24	25	26
27	28	29	30	31		

December
1998

January 1999						
S	M	T	W	T	F	S
					1	2
3	4	5	6	7	8	9
10	11	12	13	14	15	16
17	18	19	20	21	22	23
24	25	26	27	28	29	30
31						

Sunday
20
Ramadan begins
___

Monday
21

Rebecca West, b. 1892
___

Tuesday
22

Winter Solstice, 1:56 am EST
___

Wednesday
23

Giuseppe di Lampedusa, b. 1896
___

Thursday
24

Juan Ramón Jiménez, b. 1881
Matthew Arnold, b. 1822
___

Friday
25

Christmas Day
___

Saturday
26   Kwanzaa   Jean Toomer, b. 1894   Henry Miller, b. 1891

December						
S	M	T	W	T	F	S
		1	2	3	4	5
6	7	8	9	10	11	12
13	14	15	16	17	18	19
20	21	22	23	24	25	26
27	28	29	30	31		

December
1998

January 1999						
S	M	T	W	T	F	S
					1	2
3	4	5	6	7	8	9
10	11	12	13	14	15	16
17	18	19	20	21	22	23
24	25	26	27	28	29	30
31						

Rebecca West
December 21, 1892 - March 15, 1983

She believed that "any authentic work of art must start an argument between the artist and his audience." Her magnum opus about Yugoslavia, *Black Lamb and Grey Falcon*, continues to inspire debate. Critic Diana Trilling named it one of "the very greatest books of the last 50 years," but journalist John Gunther said it was "not so much a book about Yugoslavia as a book about Rebecca West."

And who was she? Born in County Kerry, Ireland, she was christened Cicily Isabel Fairfield, but she rejected this name out of Victorian romance and took as her nom de plume Rebecca West, the heroine of *Rosmersholm*, by Henrik Ibsen.

In a career that spanned 70 years, she wrote four collections of essays and seven novels, and reams of journalism. Wallace Shawn of *The New Yorker*, where much of her reportage appeared, called her a "giant." She was often compared to George Bernard Shaw, who quipped that she "could handle a pen as brilliantly as ever I could and much more savagely."

Like Shaw, she wrote fearlessly, with a kind of Olympian assurance. "Writers on the subject of August Strindberg," she asserted, "have hitherto omitted to mention that he could not write." About feminism, she said, "People call me a feminist whenever I express sentiments that differentiate me from a doormat or a prostitute." About White House aides during Watergate, she opined that they "all look like the handsome, grown-up grandchildren of the plastic gnomes that ornament certain gardens."

And she described H. G. Wells (who fathered her only child and was her lover for ten years) as an "old maid among novelists." Besotted at first by her "dark, expressive, troubled eyes" and "big soft mouth," Wells discovered that Rebecca West had a "splendid disturbed brain."

Forced to raise her son alone, West called motherhood "that cruel failure of the human structure." All her life she spoke out against the identification of female virtue with passivity. In 1936, she wrote an open letter to the Peace Pledge Union, asking, "Do you believe that you are going to abolish Cancer if you get 100,000 people to sign a pledge that they do not intend to have Cancer?"

Even at 90, just months before her death, she refused to draw a veil over reality. She told *Vogue* magazine, "It is not that you have any fears about your own death, it is that your upholstery is already dead around you."

The Bible

It is the most famous piece of writing in the Western world. A sacred text for Judaism, Christianity, and, indirectly, Islam, it is at once the foundation of Western culture and a deeply moving record of human experience.

Its influence on language and the arts is unrivalled. Northrop Frye calls the Bible "the great code" of Western literature. Through its King James Version, in particular, it has shaped the English language. Phrases from Scripture

Johann Gutenberg pulls a first proof of the Bible printed with moveable type.

riddle our everyday conversation: "the apple of his eye," "the skin of my teeth," "the salt of the earth."

The oldest surviving manuscripts of the Bible were written hundreds of years after the original texts were composed. Of the authors and redactors of those first texts we know little, except what can be gleaned from their words. Harold Bloom suggests that the anonymous author of the Hebrew Scriptures—the "teller of the tales" of Jacob and Joseph, Moses and the Exodus—is "the great original of the literary and oral traditions ... a writer more inescapable than Shakespeare and more pervasive in our consciousness than Freud."

More anthology than narrative, the Bible has no common style—although the King James Version has led many to believe otherwise—but is rather a miscellany of themes, stories, and literary forms that by the 4th century C.E. comprised a virtually inviolable canon. Peruse the Scriptures, and one finds narrative, parable, patriotic poetry, allegory, and texts—such as the Psalms—drawn from liturgical ceremony. Nearly every sort of literary effect is employed, from metaphor and hyperbole to personification, irony, and symbolism.

In the West, the earliest Christians read a Latin Bible translated from original Greek and Hebrew manuscripts. In the East, Greek became the biblical language of choice. With the invention of the printing press and the onset of the Protestant Reformation in the 15th and 16th centuries, translators began rendering the Bible in the languages of common people. For their efforts, some paid a steep price. The author of the first English translation of the Bible, William Tyndale, was put to death as a heretic by the Catholic Inquisition in 1536.

In the beginning was the Word. And words followed. Themes, characters, plots, and imagery from the Bible underpin much of Western literature. Its rhythms bolster our prose. "The Lord gave the word," sings the poet David, in his Psalms. "Great was the company of those that published it."

Sunday
27

Monday
28

Boxing Day

Tuesday
29

Wednesday
30

Thursday
31

 Friday
1

Catherine Drinker Bowen, b. 1897   New Year's Day

Saturday
2

December

S	M	T	W	T	F	S
		1	2	3	4	5
6	7	8	9	10	11	12
13	14	15	16	17	18	19
20	21	22	23	24	25	26
27	28	29	30	31		

December 1998
January 1999

January 1999

S	M	T	W	T	F	S
					1	2
3	4	5	6	7	8	9
10	11	12	13	14	15	16
17	18	19	20	21	22	23
24	25	26	27	28	29	30
31						

Selected Sources

Barnes, Eric Wollencott. *The Lady of Fashion: The Life and the Theatre of Anna Cora Mowatt*. New York: Charles Scribner's Sons, 1954.

Bieber, Konrad. *Simone de Beauvoir*. Boston: Twayne Publishers, 1979.

Bloom, Harold, Introduction to *Modern Critical Views. The Bible*. Edited and with an introduction by Harold Bloom. New York: Chelsea House Publishers, 1987. Pages 1-14.

Born, Franz. *Jules Verne: The Man Who Invented the Future*. Englewood Cliffs, New Jersey: Prentice-Hall, Inc., 1964.

Bullock, Alan. *Natalia Ginzburg*. New York/Oxford: Berg Publishers, 1991.

Christian, William A., Jr. *Moving Crucifixes in Modern Spain*. Princeton, New Jersey: Princeton Unversity Press, 1992.

Coles, Gladys Mary. *Mary Webb*. Bridgend, Mid Glamorgan: Seren Books/Poetry Wales Press, 1990.

Cthulhu 2000. A Lovecraftian Anthology. Edited by Jim Turner. Sauk City, Wisconsin: Arkham House Publishers, 1995.

Dalven, Rae. *Anna Comnena*. New York: Twayne Publishers, 1972.

Dennison, Sally. *(Alternative) Literary Publishing: Five Modern Histories*. Iowa City: University of Iowa Press, 1984.

Dillon, Millicent. *A Little Original Sin: The Life and Work of Jane Bowles*. New York: Anchor Books, Doubleday, 1982.

Douglas, Ann. *Terrible Honesty*. New York: Farrar, Straus and Giroux, 1995.

Dowden, Steve. "The Man Who Would Be Goethe." *The New York Times Book Review*. November 12, 1995.

Egerton, George, ed. *Political Memoir: Essays on the Politics of Memory*. London: Frank Cass, 1994.

Ellmann, Richard. *James Joyce*. New York and Oxford: Oxford University Press, 1983.

Emblen, D.L. *Peter Mark Roget: The Word and the Man*. New York: Thomas Y. Crowell Company, 1970.

Furia, Philip. *Ira Gershwin*. New York and Oxford: Oxford University Press, 1996.

Gabel, John B., and Charles B. Wheeler. *The Bible as Literature: An Introduction*. 2nd ed. New York: Oxford University Press, 1990.

Gilman, Charlotte Perkins. *The Yellow Wallpaper and Other Writings*. With an Introduction by Lynne Sharon Schwartz. New York: Bantam Books, 1989.

Gordon, Mary. "Surviving History." *The New York Times Magazine*. March 25, 1990.

Gottcent, John H. *The Bible: A Literary Study*. Boston: Twayne Publishers, 1986.

Gray, Francine du Plessix. *Rage and Fire: A Life of Louise Colet, Pioneer Feminist, Literary Star, Flaubert's Muse*. New York: Simon & Schuster, 1994.

Hanne, Michael. Introduction to *Literature and Travel*. Atlanta, GA: Rodopi, 1993. Pages 3-7.

Heineman, Helen. *Frances Trollope*. Boston: Twayne Publishers, 1984.

Hinnant, Charles H. *Thomas Hobbes*. Boston: Twayne Publishers, 1977.

Jean, George. *Writing: The Story of Alphabets and Scripts*. Translated by Jenny Oates. New York: Harry N. Abrams, 1992.

Joshi, S. T. *H. P. Lovecraft: A Life*. West Warwick, RI: Necromonicon Press, 1996.

Kazantzakis, Helene. *Nikos Kazantzakis. A Biography Based on His Letters*. New York: Simon and Schuster, 1968.

Kazantzakis, Nikos. *The Odyssey: A Modern Sequel*. Translation into English verse, introduction, synopsis and notes by Kimon Friar. New York: Simon and Schuster, 1958.

Kenny, Vincent S. *Paul Green*. New York: Twayne Publishers, 1971.

Lane, Ann J. *To Herland and Beyond: The Life and Work of Charlotte Perkins Gilman*. New York: Pantheon Books, 1990.

Lefer, Diane. *Emma Lazarus*. New York: Chelsea House Publishers, 1988.

Levy, Eugene. *James Weldon Johnson: Black Leader, Black Voice*. Chicago and London: University of Chicago Press, 1973.

Loos, Anita. *Kiss Hollywood Good-bye*. New York: The Viking Press, 1974.

Lovecraft, H.P. and August Derleth. *The Watchers Out of Time and Others*. Sauk City, Wisconsin: Arkham House Publishers, 1974.

Malcolm X. *The Autobiography of Malcolm X*. As told to Alex Haley. New York: Ballantine Books, n.d.

Marks, Elaine. "Simone de Beauvoir." *Dictionary of Literary Biography*. Vol. 72. Detroit: Gale Research, Inc. Pages 42-57.

May Sarton. *Woman and Poet*. Edited by Constance Hunting. Orono, Maine: National Poetry Foundation, Inc., University of Maine, 1982.

Morris, Roy Jr. *Ambrose Bierce: Alone in Bad Company.* New York: Crown Publishers, 1995.

Oates, Joyce Carol. "The King of Weird." *The New York Review of Books.* Volume XLIII, Number 17.

Pattison, Walter T. *Emilia Pardo Bazàn.* New York: Twayne Publishers, 1971.

Pawel, Ernst. *The Poet Dying: Heinrich Heine's Last Years in Paris.* New York: Farrar, Straus and Giroux, 1995.

Peters, Margot. *May Sarton. A Biography.* New York: Alfred A. Knopf, 1997.

Plimpton, George, ed. *The Writer's Chapbook: A Compendium of Fact, Opinion, Wit, and Advice from the 20th Century's Preeminent Writers.* New York: Viking, 1990.

Prose, Francine. "Expatriate Games." Travel Section. *The New York Times.* March 3, 1996.

Ransom, Teresa. *Fanny Trollope. A Remarkable Life.* Foreword by Victoria Glendinning. New York: St. Martin's Press, 1995.

Reichardt, Mary R. *A Web of Relationship: Women in the Short Fiction of Mary Wilkins Freeman.* Jackson and London: University Press of Mississippi, 1992.

Sheehy, Helen. *Eva Le Gallienne.* New York: Alfred A. Knopf, 1996.

Sherman, Susan. *May Sarton Among the Usual Days: A Portrait.* Unpublished poems, letters, journals, and photographs selected and edited by Susan Sherman with a Preface by May Sarton. New York: W. W. Norton & Company, 1993.

Snodgrass, Mary Ellen. *Late Achievers: Famous People Who Succeeded Late in Life.* Englewood, Colorado: Libraries Unlimited, 1992.

Stanford, W. B. *The Ulysses Theme.* Ann Arbor: The University of Michigan Press, 1968.

Sweetman, David. *Mary Renault.* New York: Harcourt Brace & Company, 1993.

Tillinghast, Richard. *Robert Lowell's Life and Work: Damaged Grandeur.* Ann Arbor: The University of Michigan Press, 1995.

TriQuarterly 56. Winter 1983. Editor Reginald Gibbons. Northwestern University, Evanston, Ilinois.

Vircondelete, Alain. *Duras: A Biography.* Translated by Thomas Buckley. Normal, IL: Dalkey Archive Press/Illinois State University, 1994.

Wolff, Larry. "The 20th Century: Dr. Schnitzler's Diagnosis," *The New York Times Book Review,* November 8, 1992. Page 1.

Ziolkowski, Theodore. "Lord of the Antinomies." *The New York Times Book Review.* March 26, 1995.

Photo and Illustration Credits

Many of the photographs reproduced in this book come from the collections of the Library of Congress, Washington, D.C.

The authors wish to acknowledge the following additional sources of photographs and illustrations:

About the Authors

The authors of "On Writers and Writing" are both biographers. Helen Sheehy is the author of *Margo: The Life and Theatre of Margo Jones*, (Southern Methodist University Press, 1989) and *Eva Le Gallienne* (Alfred A. Knopf, 1996). She is working on a biography of Eleonora Duse. A resident of Connecticut, Sheehy has written a theater textbook, a number of articles and essays, and has taught theater for over twenty-five years.

Leslie Stainton lives in Michigan and is at work on a biography of Federico Garcia Lorca for which she received a two-year Fulbright Research Grant. Her articles and essays have appeared in various newspapers and periodicals including the *New York Times*, the *Washington Post*, and *American Theatre* magazine.

Index

An alphabetical listing of writers or essay subjects and the week in which they appear.